TABLE OF CONTENTS

Chapter 9 - One Hand Operation 161

Appendix

Chapter 1

PREPARING TO PREVAIL

AUTHOR'S MESSAGE

 Defensive Handgun was written to help law abiding citizens enhance their knowledge on safe firearm handling and provide them with a platform to build solid defensive handgun skills. Many people buy handguns due to safety concerns for themselves or their loved ones. Without fundamental training in safe handling, gun owners risk creating dangerous situations instead of providing protective conditions.

Despite the number of legally owned firearms, most law abiding citizens are ill trained to deal with life threatening confrontations. It is critically important that handgun owners master simple, repeatable defensive countermeasures that can help them survive violent encounters. This book demonstrates tactical applications for handgun safety and use. Defensive Handgun employs a straightforward approach designed to show readers how to maximize their control in life threatening situations by effectively using fundamental handgun skills. Knowledge is an owner's real power when handling a handgun and that's what I want you to have.

Please enjoy the reading and take time to master the techniques at the range. I encourage you to master them first and judge them later. Stay safe and may God continue to bless and watch over you and your family.

As always special blessings go out to my daughter Jasmyne, who is the love of my life and the inspiration that keeps me motivated and focused. May everyone be so blessed to have a daughter as loving, caring and beautiful as she! May you use the special love of a parent as your motivation to increase your protection skills so that you may continue to watch over and protect those you love. Also thanks to Lana Fallon and Mike Smith. Mike is my best friend, who has worked closely with me on countless protection details and the guy who always has my six). May God continue to bless you and your families!

Disclaimer & Release from Liability

- The information contained in this book is designed to help you increase your knowledge in safe firearms handling; provide you with a platform upon which to build your shooting skills; provide you some practical defensive techniques; and give you a broad overview of some key Georgia Firearm Codes.

- The Georgia Firearm Codes included are not all inclusive and you are encouraged to read the entire Georgia Codes and consult with your attorney as to their actual meaning.

- This book is under no circumstances to be viewed as a restatement of the law in any jurisdiction or to assure compliance with any applicable federal, state or local laws, ordinances, rules or regulations. You must consult a local attorney to ascertain compliance with all applicable federal, state or local laws, ordinances rules or regulations.

- Firearms, shooting, and training are potentially dangerous and can lead to serious injury or death. Discharging firearms in poorly ventilated areas, cleaning firearms, or handling lead or lead containing reloading components may result in exposure to lead. Wash hands after handling ammunition or discharging your firearm.

- Each and every person involved in firearms training should act as a safety officer and be constantly alert to any potential safety violations. Care and safe handling is essential.

- By receiving and/or reviewing this book, subsequent

classroom or range training you agree to not hold the author, instructors, trainers, publishers or company liable for its contents and your subsequent use of the materials or techniques discussed.

- You hereby release the author, instructors, trainers, publishers and company harmless and release them from liabilities, any cause of action, civil or criminal, which may result due to the use or misuse negligence, misconduct, of the course materials and its instructions.

You and only you are responsible and liable for your actions.

Firearms Liability

This book is designed for the readers and students of our instructional training sessions to understand some critical firearms liability areas.

- Responsibility for your actions – you and only you are responsible for your actions.

- Discharging your firearm – we should all understand when we discharge our firearms; we are responsible for those rounds until they stop (and even after that). That is why constant training, care and discretion should be used whenever we take a shot. Every round that misses your target puts yourself and others at risk. Always know what is behind and around your target.

- Lost or stolen firearms – Should be reported to the police and your insurance company immediately. A copy of that report and record should be kept for your own protection.

- Children – all firearms should be stored away from children. One should take advantage of as many countermeasures as possible (unload your firearms, separate them from the ammunition, apply gun locks to your firearms, place firearms in a gun safe or other secure containers).

- Straw Buyers – straw buyers are people who make firearms purchases for people who are not authorized to buy a firearm.

Care should be taken when considering purchasing a firearm for someone else or when selling a firearm. Many states limit private firearms sales and require sales to be made through firearms dealers. That allows further scrutiny by officials, particularly when a gun is sold on consignment or by the respective consignment dealer. Selling your firearm though a dealer helps reduce your potential exposure and liability.

Basic Firearm Safety

1. Treat all guns as if they are always loaded. Even when you just unloaded them, treat them as if they're loaded.

2. Never point the muzzle at anything you aren't willing to destroy!

3. Keep your finger off the trigger except when ready to shoot.

4. Watch what is in the background of your target in case you miss. What is going to stop the round if and when you fire?

Range Safety

Below are basic fundamentals of range safety:

- No alcohol allowed at the range or consumed prior to coming to the range.

- Eye and ear protection should be worn at all times.

- Weapons should be unloaded prior to entering the range.

- No loaded weapons are allowed in the classroom or any other place at the range except on the firing line.

- Load weapon only on command (cold range).

- All weapons must always be pointed down-range (Down-range is the direction of the targets).

- When not on the firing line, all weapons should have the action visibly open.

- NEVER point your weapon anywhere other than at the ground and the target/backstop/butts/pits (all are different terms for where the targets are).

- Keep finger off of the trigger except when ready to fire.

- Shoot only at the assigned targets.

- No dry firing allowed behind the firing line.

- Never move forward of the firing line for any reason...If you drop anything forward of the line, (including ammo, targets, your firearm etc.) – notify the range officer.

- If your weapon jams, fails to fire or misfires, place it on the range bench rest pointing down range and contact the range officer.

- No horseplay of any type will be tolerated.

COMMONLY USED RANGE TERMS

- Hot Range – a range where guns are expected to be loaded all the time without commands to "reload" by the range officer.

- Cold Range – a range where guns are unloaded most of the time and only loaded and reloaded by the direction of the range officer.

- Danger Zone – anything in front of the line of fire or where you must keep you weapon pointed whenever it is out of the holster.

- Safe Zone – everything behind the line of fire. This is where you want to keep all of your body parts. Avoid having your weapon un-holstered or pointed in the safe zone.

THINGS TO KNOW AS YOU PREPARE TO TRAIN

Where do you want to concentrate your training?

- More than 80% of gunfights occur within a 7 yard distance. Over half of those happened within 5 feet or less!

- 15% of fights occur at distances exceeding 50 feet.

- Gunfights tend to be sudden and violent. The estimated elapsed time is roughly 3 seconds.

- About 70% of gunfights occur in reduced light environments.

- Almost 50% of the time you might face more than one assailant.

- Most handgun encounters tend to be pretty fast, violent and conclusive. They are often over in 3 shots or less.

When it comes to handgun carry and selection, I am a large fan of shooting the largest caliber you can shoot accurately; whether that is a 38, 9 mm, .40, .45 or any other caliber in between. A big gun that you cannot shoot accurately does you little good. The key must make sure your shots are having a positive ballistic effect on your target or adversary.

Definitional Clarity

Before we move forward with talking about firearms, protection or survival, I think it is important to get some situational clarity on the focus of our training and preparation. Two words of critical importance are *defensive* and *tactics*. Below let's take a look at how the dictionary describes the two:

Defensive

Adjective

1. Intended or appropriate for defending: protective.

2. a. Intended to withstand or deter aggression or attack.
   b. Of or relating to the effort prevent an opponent from gaining points in a game or athletic contest.
   c. Performed so as to avoid risk, danger or legal liability.

3. Of or relating to defense.

Noun

1. A means of defense.

2. An attitude or position defense.

Tactics

NOUN

1. a. The military science that deals with securing objectives
    set by strategy, especially the technique of deploying and
    directing troops, ships and aircraft in effective maneuvers
    against an enemy.
    b. Maneuvers used against an enemy.

2. A procedure or set of maneuvers engaged to achieve an
    end, an aim or a goal.

First and foremost I want to make it abundantly clear that self-defense is not a sport, and Defensive Handgun is not about the sport of shooting. It is about helping you build a solid defense platform to assist you in saving your life or that of a loved one. Our primary goal is to help you withstand, deter or prevail against an act of aggression, particularly deadly force situations. It is an unfortunate reality that most people are ill prepared to effectively defend themselves from a planned attack without proper training. The primary focus is to help expose you to tactics and tools which are designed to help you survive a tactical or defensive encounter. As we think about preparing to train we will focus on elements of defensive as well as tactical application. Remember simplicity leads to consistency. Consistency leads to competency. Efficiency translates into speed. You must be both competent and efficient to enhance your ability to prevail.

People often try to complicate the activities associated with a tactical situation or gun fight. There are four things which typically occur in a tactical situation, you are either:

1. Maintaining your position behind cover

2. Shooting

3. Moving

4. Reloading

If you are not doing some combination of the above you are probably dying! You don't want to be a spectator in a gun or knife fight. In the following chapter we will focus on understanding the mindset, the tools and training required to help enhance your defensive platform and protective capabilities.

The Mindset To Prevail

The first phase of any defensive or tactical platform involves developing the proper mindset. Simply stated you must first and foremost believe you will prevail. You must be more motivated than your potential attacker to get away, protect yourself or your family and/or neutralize the threat. You must learn to harness the energy and power from the body's *fight* or *flight* response rather than freezing under pressure. It will take both physical and mental conditioning to allow you to harness your adrenaline and channel it into proper action. Mental confidence and toughness, can provide you a decisive advantage in a violent encounter. However the mindset without defensive skills is hallucination!

When confronted with the threat of violence the mind typically goes through a series of steps before choosing a response. Those actions commonly fall into one of the three areas:

1. Threat Recognition – in analyzing a potentially violent situation, the mind must first recognize danger before it can start to process it.

2. Situation Exploration – once the mind recognizes the danger, the mind quickly considers available courses of action.

3. Moment of Reaction – after processing the danger's potential outcomes, and considering possible courses of action, the mind then propels the body into action,. In some cases *paralysis of inaction.*

Training accelerates your actions by allowing you to quickly assess violent situations. It also ingrains the appropriate responses and activates your countermeasures.

Situational Readiness

"All attacks happen at the same time – NOW!" It is important that we maintain a state of situational readiness. This should not be confused with a state of paranoia, as paranoia often causes us to freeze or not accurately access our situation; which may lead to an undesirable and/or a tragic outcome. It is important that we maintain a state of alertness or awareness. We should also learn to separate risks from threats. Risks are things we often have some level of control over:

- Going to an ATM machine in the middle of the night

- Parking next to a van at the mall (particularly when we are by alone)

- Sitting in a car balancing our checkbook before going into the store

- Sitting in a car and reading your mail while waiting to pick up your child from school or practice

- Parking on a dark street one block over, as opposed to paying a $3 or $5 valet charge while visiting a restaurant or night club

- Flashing large sums of money

- Wearing flashy jewelry in underprivileged neighborhoods or countries

- Pulling up directly behind the car in front of you (not being able to see their rear tires) and not giving yourself room to evade a carjacker

- Failing to reset your alarm once you enter the house or at minimum when you retire for the evening.

Threats are potential hazards we face that we have little to no control over (i.e.):

- Criminals
- Carjackers
- Deranged Individuals
- Disgruntled Employees
- Rapist
- Home Invaders
- Stalkers
- Terrorists

As we go through our day to day routines it is important that we remain in touch with not just our surroundings but also the people who are interacting in the environment with us. Consider whether anyone's actions seem inappropriate for the situation.

- Long or heavy coat during a warm day (could their coat be hiding something)

- Large bulges beneath their clothes (is it a cell phone or a weapon)

- Hands constantly under their shirt or in their pockets

- Someone who avoids making eye contact

- Someone who appears to be startled by your presence

- Someone whose actions are triggered off by yours

- Someone who is looking to start a major argument over what appears to be a very insignificant matter

Definitional Clarity

STAT•IC - ADJECTIVE

1. pertaining to or characterized by a fixed position

2. showing little or no change

3. lacking movement, development or vitality

Static training is typically helpful in assisting you with the building of fundamental firearm skills. This is the type of training most people do at most indoor and outdoor ranges. Helps build basic skills but rarely simulates the environment most people face in personal protection situations (moving, getting off line, working from cover, working from concealment, presentation/the draw etc.), as most ranges restrict or severely limit that type of training for safety reasons.

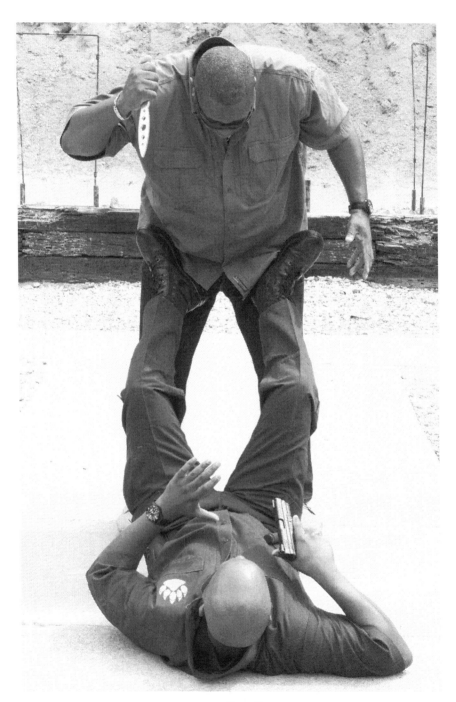

Dʏ•ɴᴀᴍ•ɪᴄ — ᴀᴅᴊᴇᴄᴛɪᴠᴇ

pertaining to or characterized by energy, or effective action; vigorously active or forceful; energetic.

physics
1. of or pertaining to force or power
2. of or pertaining to force related to motion

"When a crisis occurs, we very rarely rise to meet the occasion in truth; we merely default to our training!" Dynamic training is designed to help you advance your firearm skills and better simulate the type of environment you might actually experience in a firearm encounter. When a gun is pointed at you or you point a weapon at someone else one of four things typically occurs:

• We or they comply (either actual or faux compliance) with the commands of the person holding the gun.

- We or they attempt to move (trying to move to cover or execute a tactical escape).

- We or they attempt to return fire while moving or working from concealment.

- Someone gets seriously injured or dies.

So unlike the static training we do at most ranges, the target will probably be moving, we will probably be moving or some combination of the above. So consequently limiting your training to static range training will typically give you a false sense of your abilities.

Chapter 2

SELECTING YOUR TOOLS

WHY DO WE OWN HANDGUNS?

There are multiple reasons people purchase handguns. Below are six of the more common reasons consumers purchase firearms:

- Collecting
- Competitive Shooting
- Duty
- Hunting
- Personal Protection
- Recreational Shooting

I to be very clear in intent of this book. It is not designed to focus on the art of collecting, competitive shooting, hunting or recreational shooting, but to give you practical handgun fundamentals which will aid you in any type of shooting. Moreover I intend to give you some common sense defense counter measures for Duty or Personal Protection.

Selecting a Handgun

Things to consider when selecting a handgun:

- What am I buying this handgun for?

- Will it be primarily used for personal carry, home protection or a duty weapon?

- If this is a duty weapon are there specific departmental considerations I must take into account (i.e. double action only)?

- Other than me who else in my household may use this weapon?

- How much training will I and the other members of my household who may use this firearm be able to devote to training?

- Is the caliber appropriate for my intended application?

- Would my family's, my departments' or my personal needs, be better satisfied through multiple firearms, as opposed to one size fits all?

Generally the major considerations when it comes to selecting a firearm, particularly for self defense should be Reliability, Simplicity, Accuracy and Caliber.

- Reliability – when it comes to reliability most of the larger modern gun makers build reliable hand guns.

- Simplicity – ease of operation (trigger, magazine release, slide release, and takedown…takedown is important when it comes to keeping your weapon clean), should be a major consideration. In the stress free life of the square range every handgun seems fine. Under the stress of a deadly force situation you need a weapon that is simple to operate, and one you feel you can operate effectively under low light conditions.

- Accuracy - is a direct byproduct of training and the component you can most impact. Most of today's larger modern gun manufacturer's weapons shoot pretty reliable groups from any gun vise, so accuracy is not about the gun, but about the operator. Most guns shoot more accurately than you can hold them.

- Caliber – consider shooting the largest caliber and heaviest load of bullet that you can shoot accurately. Accuracy should always trump caliber size. For personal protection I am not a fan of any caliber below 9mm (although well placed rounds to the vital areas from most calibers will typically have the desired effect on your adversary). The first consideration of accuracy is your ability to place two rounds repeatedly center-mass. If your thoughts extend beyond that, then you are typically working from a more advanced mindset and have made the mental commitment to dedicate more time to your personal defense training.

In general a revolver's inherent advantages lie in its simplicity, and ease of operations with minimal potential for jams. Semi-automatic handguns advantages typically lie in their increased ammunition capacity and speed in reloading for most operators. Consider testing multiple calibers in both revolvers and semi-automatic pistols before making a purchase (*many reputable ranges typically offer both revolvers and semi-automatic that you can rent by the hour prior making a purchase*).

Material choices generally include titanium, aluminum alloy, steel, and stainless steel. Finishes, primarily for alloys or steel, include matte (non-reflective black), blued (mirror-like blue-black), and nickel plated (shiny silver chrome).

Stainless steel resists rusting, blued steel is extremely durable but will corrode if not cared for, and titanium and aluminum alloy are extremely light, with titanium being the lightest (about two-thirds the weight of steel). Materials and finishes are generally a matter of preference.

After these considerations, now ask yourself, would my needs be best served by a revolver or a semi-automatic pistol?

UNDERSTANDING YOUR HANDGUN

At the conclusion of this section you will understand the critical parts and functionality of a revolver and/or semi-auto pistol. They will also understand key considerations in selecting a firearm:

The Revolver

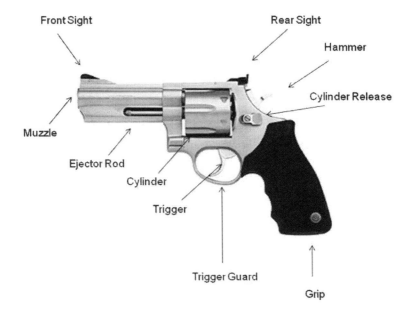

Front Sight
Rear Sight
Hammer
Cylinder Release
Muzzle
Ejector Rod
Cylinder
Trigger
Trigger Guard
Grip

COMMONLY PURCHASED REVOLVERS

- Colt
- Dan Wesson
- Ruger
- Smith and Wesson
- Taurus

The Semi-Automatic Pistol

Commonly Purchased Semi-Automatic Pistols

- Beretta
- Colt
- FN
- Glock
- H&K
- Ruger
- Kimber
- Sig Sauer
- Smith and Wesson
- Springfield
- Taurus

Selecting a Holster

At the conclusion of this section you will understand the key considerations to assist you in selecting a holster. What were the criteria you used when you selected your holster?

No one single holster will work for all situations. Things you may want to consider when selecting a holster:

- Will this be used for exposed carry or concealed carry?
- Body type
- Lifestyle
- Activity Level
- Retention requirements
- Comfort

- Types of Materials
- Would my needs be better satisfied through multiple holster acquisitions?

 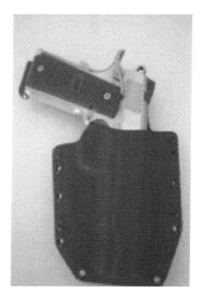

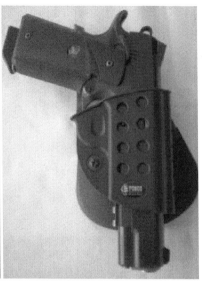

As an example my primary preference for a material type is leather under normal conditions. However when I have to work in extremely hot and humid conditions I prefer some type of synthetic material (Kydex) so the salt content of my sweat does not break down my leather holster over time. If you are working exposed carry retention buttons or straps are highly encouraged;

however if you are carrying concealed that may be less of a concerned (as no one should know you are carrying, but you).

Styles

- Ankle
- Belly Bands
- Belt side
- Cross Draw
- Drop Leg
- Inside the Pants
- Middle of the Back
- Paddle
- Pocket
- Shoulder (Rigs or T-Shirts)

Carry positions and styles may vary based on activity level, dexterity of carrier, clothing and/or duty requirements. Examples:

- While appendix carry is often the most accessible position for most people under normal concealed carry conditions, it is not good for people who normally embrace (hug), when they greet others.

- Kidney carry is often beneficial for some as it places your weapon further to the side and behind you, so if your sport coat accidently blouse open, your weapon is not instantly visible, however this position may not work well for those with limited dexterity.

- When carrying in cold climates many carriers may opt for shoulder rigs or cross draw holsters as people often stand with their hands crossed which places their strong side hand in close proximity to their weapon in a relaxed low profile look.

Materials

- Carbon Fiber
- Cotton
- Injection Molded Composite
- Kydex
- Leather
- Nylon

UNDERSTANDING AMMUNITION

At the conclusion of this section you will understand the key components which make up a cartridge. Understand the uses and performance characteristics of some of the most popular bullets and different types of cartridges:

Cartridge Components

- Bullet – the actual projectile which is expelled from the firearm.
- Cartridge Case – is the actual housing which contains the

bullet, gunpowder and primer.

- Gunpowder or propellant – any various powders used to expel the projectile from the casing, often made of potassium nitrate, charcoal, and sulfur.

- Primer – a cap or a tube containing a small amount of explosive used to ignite the main explosive charge used in a firearm.

Types of Cartridges

- Rimfire – primer is contained in the rim outer-edges of the bottom of the base
- Centerfire – primer is located in the middle of the bottom base of the cartridge

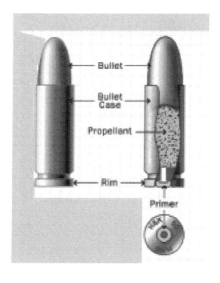

Popular Bullet Types

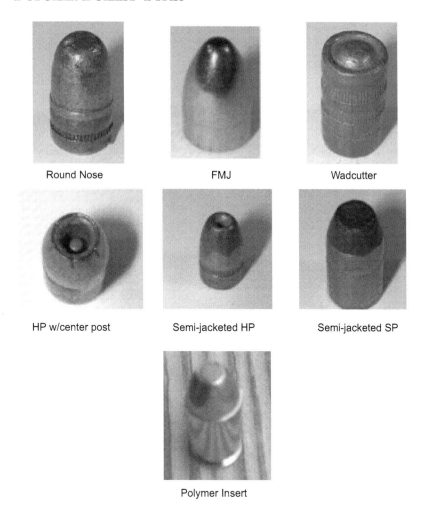

Round Nose	FMJ	Wadcutter
HP w/center post	Semi-jacketed HP	Semi-jacketed SP
	Polymer Insert	

Just as building a house is easier with the right tools. So is firearm operation; the same care that went into selecting your firearm should go into selecting your ammunition. The most common considerations in selecting ammunition should be safety, purpose, reliability, accuracy and recoil. Later you will learn than many weapon malfunctions are caused by poor quality ammunition.

- Round Nose Bullets – this bullet is composed 100% of lead, typically used for target shooting, very economical and provides enhance ballistic capabilities compared to that of the Wadcutter.

- Full Metal Jacket – often referred to as hardball, the tops and sides of this bullet are contained in a hard metal jacket, usually consisting of an alloy of copper or occasionally mild steel. The base of the bullet is open exposing a lead core. The bullet is designed to minimize expansion or deformation. Often used by the military particularly in small arms warfare.

- Wadcutter – this bullet is lead constructed however the top of the bullet comes to the top of the casing of the cartridge and does not protrude above it. Often used by revolver target shooters, due to the clean hole they make in paper targets. Typically one of the most economical bullets you can purchase.

- Hollow point with center post – this bullet has a central rod in the center of the bullet and is designed to enhance expansion on impact. Often used in personal protection to reduce over-penetration.

- Semi-jacketed hollow point – this bullet is similar to the JHP, but the jacket does not completely cover the lead core. A small section of core at the top of the bullet is left exposed. This is often common in older bullets designed for .38 special, .357 and .44 magnum calibers.

- Semi-jacketed soft point – this bullet is a hybrid of the full metal jacket and soft point. The jacketed components to aid in penetration but provide more delayed expansion properties.

- Polymer insert – this bullet is designed to prevent the hollow-point cavity from being clogged with fibers and other materials, which can inhibit reliable bullet expansion (i.e. Corbon Powerball, Hornady Critical Defense). This bullet is often used in personal defense.

- Higher pressure or plus "+P" or "+P+" ammunition should only be used in firearms certified for them (check your owner's manual).

Cleaning your Handgun

When a firearm is fired it accumulates dirt, gunpowder residue and other foreign particulars which may make your firearm prone to malfunctions, corrosion or unnecessary wear if not properly maintained. Firearms left unattended or stored for long periods of time may also become susceptible to dirt and dust which can also adversely impact operations.

Before cleaning, first make sure your firearm is unloaded! Now check it again to make sure it is unloaded! Remove all ammunition and store it securely in a separate room.

- Field Strip Firearm (please refer to your owner's manual).

- Wear safety glasses and latex gloves during cleaning.

- Clean regularly with some type of solvent (Break Free, Hoppes etc), cotton patches, bore snakes, nylon or wire brushes, jags, bore rods.

- Lubricate with a light gun oil after cleaning (check your owner's manual for the recommended type)

- Wipe down the outside of your firearm with a gun friendly cloth suitable for your type of firearm (Kleen-Bore Silicone Gun Reel Cloth).

- If storing please store your handgun empty and out of the reach of unintended users (all firearms should be stored unloaded, with trigger locks and then stored in a locked container or safe whenever possible).

Keep your firearm clean and lubricated. This is a major tool to assist you in protecting your family or other team members. Your job should be to help minimize the potential for weapons malfunctions caused by dirty or poor conditioned weapons.

Handgun Accessories

There are a number of accessories which one can consider for your defensive or tactical handgun. One of the most important considerations is to keep your Handgun as functionally simple as possible. Any high-tech modifications should not come at the expense of simplicity. The modifications should help make your handgun easier to operate. You must also ask yourself, if you are considering any high-tech modifications, can I still operate the handgun effectively if the high-tech devices fail or malfunction? Throughout the years one of the things that have always made the handgun and effective tools was its ease of operation in the face of danger.

ALTERNATE GRIPS

Changing your grips larger to smaller or smaller to larger is one of the easiest ways to customize your weapon to best fit you. Other considerations may be the use of grip sleeves to enhance grip or reduce recoil. A firm grip is a must; the last thing you want during a tactical engagement is your handgun slipping out of your hand.

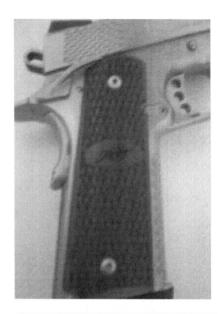

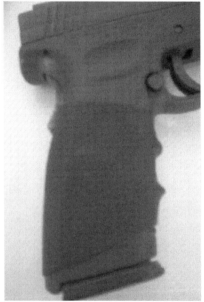

The choice of enhanced recoil reduction or not is a matter
of preference. There are a number of good choices in recoil
reduction options and companies. Hogue is one of the more well
known names.

SIGHTS

Sights are designed to make visual acquisition or slight alignment easier. Sights may range from beads, to blades, to night sights, to tritium, to red dots or holographic sights. The most important consideration should be does the sight I am considering help support the type of use I am preparing to employ this weapon for? Remember the Handgun is historically a close range weapon and most factory installed sights are typically satisfactory for most jobs.

If magnification is desired and shots and are typically going to be within 100 yards you may want to consider 2X and no more than 4X optics. Remember time is life and the faster you can get on target the better. This book is not about handgun hunting but handgun personal defense.

Reflex Sights

What they lack in magnification, reflex sights make up for with speed. Since there is effectively no parallax, once sighted in, if you can see the red dot, the bullet will find its mark regardless of how unorthodox your view through the optic or shooting position might be. Shots on moving adversaries may be enhanced and the dot is often far more precise than iron sights and far more visible in low light.

Below are some of the more familiar sight companies:

- Trijicon
- Trudot
- TruGlo
- Meprolight

Chapter 3

HANDGUN MARKSMANSHIP FUNDAMENTALS

At the conclusion of this section you will understand the 5 fundamentals of Handgun marksmanship. Like all good repeatable skills good handgun performance is built on a stable platform of strong fundamentals. Below are the keys to consistent performance:

1. Grip
2. Stance
3. Sight Alignment
4. Breath Control
5. Trigger Squeeze

THE GRIP

At the conclusion of this section you will understand the importance of a good grip and the multiple grip options available to the shooter. People often underestimate the importance of grip. Your grip is the primary thing that keeps you "one" with your weapon!

- *With your fingers and thumb making an "L," place your strong hand as high up on the grip as possible.*

- The apex of the web of your hand should be centered at the rearmost point of the curve in the gun's back strap.

- The forefinger should rest naturally along the side of the frame above the trigger and the other three fingers should wrap around easily around the front and back-strap of the grip. Imagine your *strong hand is applying pressure North to South or front to back.*

- The *strong hand thumb* may either be in a high or low position. Caution should be used in both positions:

  -Too low a position may activate the magazine release, dumping your magazine unintentionally.

  -Too high a position may induce stoppages by unintentionally dragging your thumb on the slide of a semi-automatic pistol or cylinder of a revolver.

- *Your reaction hand* should wrap naturally around your strong hand with all four fingers below the trigger guard. Imagine your reaction hand *is applying pressure East to West or side to side.*

- Your thumbs have options:

  - Thumb-lock grip – the thumb of the support hand presses down on the joint of the bent thumb of the firing hand and forms a (+), this helps bond both hands together.

  - Straight thumbs or thumbs forward – both thumbs are angled forward and ride along side of the slide of a semi-automatic handgun. This is the way most people's thumbs face when you ask them to point at something.

  - Thumbs down – this is the way most people instinctively hold a revolver or a hammer. Both thumbs are angled downward toward the ground. In single hand shooting think of the way you would hold a hammer to better understand this position. This is probably the strongest grip of all.

Grip Options

Thumbs-Lock Grip

Straight Thumbs or Thumbs Forward Grip

Thumbs Down Grip

*Proper position for
your Trigger Finger
when you are not
ready to shoot*

SHOOTING POSITIONS/STANCES

Stance

At the conclusion of this section you will understand the
importance of a good athletic stance, the multiple stances
available to you as well as the benefits of practicing multiple
stances.

- Your stance must be steady and comfortable so that you
  don't become fatigued too easily.

- Avoid locking your knees; your knees should be slightly bent.

- Your weight should be on the balls of your feet, not your
  heels or toes with a slight forward lean, avoid leaning back as
  it helps exaggerate recoil.

- Four of the more popular stances or fighting platforms are
  the Weaver, Chapman Isosceles and CAR Combat Extended;
  however any stable, athletic, and comfortable position will do.

- *Using two hands to fire is strongly encouraged whenever possible.*

Isosceles

- Body is positioned with chest square to the target or adversary.

- Weight on balls of the feet (not toes or heels).

- Feet are approximately shoulder width apart.

- Both arms are thrust out until they are locked straight forming an isosceles triangle

- Body is aggressively forward.

- Recoil is managed through the skeletal system and absorbed in the shoulders.

Advantages

- One of the simplest postures to work with.

- In concealed carry does not display strong slide in

advance of the shooting position.

- With the gun maximum distance from the head, has least amount of impact on the ears and potential ear damage.

- For that wearing body armor it maximizes the armors protective capabilities.

- Allows for easy coverage up to 180 degrees with minimum movement of your feet since neither foot leads nor trails.

Disadvantages

- Works poorly if the shooter is off balance.

- May be hard on shooters with elbow injuries.

- Tougher for people with tight fitting garments.

Weaver Stance

- The Weaver stance involves the shooter standing in a bladed position, with his or her strong side back (similar to a boxer's stance).

- In the Weaver stance, you can use your reaction hand to pull back, while pushing forward with your strong hand. This is called isometric tension and greatly aids in rapid shooting, shooting a heavy-recoiling handgun, and proper stability.

- Weight on balls of the feet (not toes or heels).

- Both arms are forward and slightly bent both elbows are down.

- Arms act as shock absorbers to aid in managing recoil.

- Gun hand pushing and reaction hand pulling back.

Advantages

- Because the arms are bent and don't extend as far it offers the shortest path from holster to line of sight.

- Because the weapon is closer to the body many shooters find it easier to track multiple targets or moving targets.

- The position makes you less of a target, whether in a shooting or fighting situation and helps protect your centerline (eyes, throat, groin, solar plexus etc.).

- Many officers prefer this position when contacting subjects as it places their weapon when holstered further away from the subject (often called the interview position).

- Often preferred by shooters with elbow injuries.

Disadvantages

- Because body is slightly bladed it opens the body up and stacks up the shooters vitals.

- For people wearing body armor it often exposes the weaker portions of the body armor (under the armpit).

Chapman Stance

- The position of the feet and body position is identical to that of the Weaver stance (body is slightly bladed to the subject or adversary).

- Strong side back.

- Weight on balls of the feet (not toes or heels).

- Strong side arm (gun side) is locked forward helps provide the sensation of a rifle stock.

- The support or reaction hand functions similar to the way one would hold and pull a rifle into your shoulder.

- Support arm is slightly bent both elbows are down.

- Arms act as shock absorbers to aid in managing recoil.

- Gun hand pushing and support hand pulling back.

Advantages

- Provides commonality for people who are use to shooting long guns.

- This stance is not dependent on body type or shape as it incorporates the use of the skeletal system and muscle mass.

- Provides the best of Weaver and Isosceles stance.

Disadvantages

- Because body is slightly bladed it opens the body up and stacks up the shooters vitals.

- For people wearing body armor it often exposes the weaker portions of the body armor (under the armpit).

SHOOTING POSITIONS

Low Ready

(Indoor

Hunt Position)

- This is a moderate to high-threat carry method.

- Designed for movement in close quarters.

- Both hands are placed on the weapon and are held approximately chest high, your elbows and the muzzle of the firearm are angled 45 degrees down toward the ground.

- Your trigger finger is indexed along side of the trigger guard.

- Safety on or off is a matter of preference, duty requirements or your level of safety consciousness.

- Reacting to a threat or adversary can be done by indexing your body on the target for extreme close quarter and delivering a shot to the adversary's mid to lower body or the shooter may chose to snap the weapon to 90 degrees to deliver the shot higher into the adversary's vitals.

- For adversaries at a distance the weapon is merely brought up to eye level to allow the shooter to focus on the sights.

Advantages

- This is a close quarter retention position and allows you to use your elbows and strikes to aid in weapon retention at close quarters.

- It allows you to protect against disarming attempts from the front, rear or flanks.

- May be utilized from a parallel or bladed position.

- Muzzle is closer to the face/eyes so it makes getting on line faster.

Disadvantages

- Because the muzzle is angled down 45 degrees, if working with a team during an entry you must avoid covering your teammates or your own body parts with the muzzle.

Compressed Ready

- This is a high-threat carry method.

- Designed for movement in close quarters.

- Both hands are placed on the weapon and are held approximately chest high, your elbows are angled 45 degrees down toward the ground.

- Your trigger finger is indexed along side of the trigger guard.

- Safety on or off is a matter of preference, duty requirements or your level of safety consciousness.

- Your initial shot will probably come from a two eyes open position.

- Reacting to a threat or adversary is done by indexing your body on the target.

- This engagement is done with little to no sight picture (this position is typically used for shots within 3 - 5 yards).

Advantages

- This is a close quarter retention position and allows you to use your elbows and strikes to aid in weapon retention at close quarters.

- It allows you to protect against disarming attempts from the front, rear or flanks.

- For those who are wearing body armor it maximizes the armors protective capabilities.

- Allows for easy coverage up to 180 degrees with minimum movement of your feet since neither foot leads nor trails.

Disadvantages

- Because body is parallel to the target or adversary it makes you a bigger target.

- Because of the absence of slight alignment it reduces your ability to make accurate shots at longer distances.

Center Axis Relock - CAR High Position

- Imagine holding your favorite beverage in the middle of your chest (solar plexus) this is where your pistol is held.

- Body perpendicular to the target.

- Strong side is back.

- Weight on balls of the feet (not toes or heels).

- The CAR high position is typically used to engage threats from 0 – 5 feet.

Advantages

- This is an extreme close quarter retention position and allows you to use your elbows for strikes to aid in weapon retention at close quarters.

- It allows you to protect against disarming attempts from the front, rear or flanks.

Disadvantages

- Because body is perpendicular to the target or adversary it opens the body up and stacks up the shooters vitals.

- For people wearing body armor it often exposes the weaker portions of the body armor (under the armpit).

- Because of the absence of slight alignment it reduces your ability to make accurate shots at longer distances.

Center Axis Relock (CAR) - Combat Extended

- This is a high threat position typically used to engage threats or adversaries from 5 feet to 10 yards.

- From the CAR High Position (weapon held about chest high/solar plexus level) rotate your gun hand elbow to about ear level.

- This will place your front sight approximately 12 – 15 inches from your eyes. This significantly aides in shooting off of your front sight as often used/encouraged in close quarter encounters.

- Body slightly bladed toward the target.

- Strong side is back.

- Weight on balls of the feet (not toes or heels).

- The gun hand has the muzzle rotated approximately 30 degrees, this helps place your bones, muscles and tendons in alignment.

- These aides in getting subsequent shots on line faster.

- Forearms are firm.

- Arms act as shock absorbers to aid in managing recoil.

- Gun hand pushing and support or reaction hand pulling back.

Advantages

- Because the arms are bent and don't extend as far it offers the shortest path from holster to line of sight.

- Because the weapon is closer to the body many shooters find it easier to track multiple targets or moving targets as the weapon more naturally follows the eyes.

- Because the arms are not extended aids in weapons retention.

- Works well from an off balanced position.

Disadvantages

- Because body is slightly bladed it opens the body up and stacks up the shooters vitals.
- For people wearing body armor it often exposes the weaker portions of the body armor (under the armpit).
- Because of the proximity to the face, it the shooter does not maintain a firm grip, the weapon could recoil into the face.

Regardless of which stance you choose the most important consideration is mobility and stability. When moving to the rear dragging your toe, helps ensure that your heel will be up if you were to bump into an obstacle and reduce your ability to fall backward.

SUPINE

If you are in this position it has probably come as the result of an "oh shit" moment. It may be the result of a trip and fall; you may have been knocked to the ground by your adversary, or from being blast into this position.

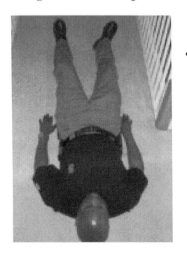

- *As you fall backwards you may want to try to fall onto your support side, or dissipate your fall. As you prepare to hit the ground try and fall onto your rear-end or at minimum your shoulder blades keeping your head forward and tucked to avoid direct contact with the ground.*

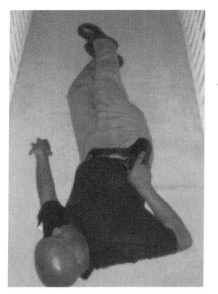

- Once you hit the ground roll onto your support side to allow you easier access to drawing your weapon. Draw your weapon index finger is positioned along the slide or below the cylinder on a revolver. Be conscious of where your muzzle is pointed (try to avoid sweeping your leg with the muzzle).

- As you roll back onto your back muzzle is then indexed toward the target or adversary. Keep your legs spread wide to avoid an intersection with your line of fire. Keep your feet angle out as you engage the threat and discharge your weapon. Try to get off of your back as soon as tactically possible.

EYE DOMINANCE

Like most dynamic activities, shooting requires good hand eye coordination. Before we can effectively work on sight alignment we must first establish if we are right or left eye dominant? Below is an exercise to help you determine your eye dominance.

While standing with your hands at your side, focus on an object out in the distance.

Now extend your hands straight out in front of you; one hand over the other (and touching) making a small quarter size hole in between your hands still focusing on the object at a distance.

Now bring your hands back toward your face, continuing to look at the object until they are only a few inches away from you face. The hole between your hands will be in front of your dominant eye (if you make a decision to shoot one eye closed, make sure the eye you keep open is your dominant eye and you work to align everything else in relation to your dominant eye).

SIGHT ALIGNMENT

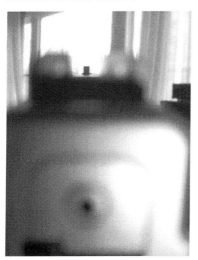 

At the conclusion of this section you will understand the importance sight alignment plays in shooting, as well as the benefits of point or instinctive shooting. You will also understand the difference between sight picture and sight alignment?

What is the difference between sight picture and sight alignment?

- Sight alignment refers to the relationship between the front sight and rear sight (should be level and centered) over dominant eye if there is no rear sight.

- Sight picture is what you see superimposed on the other end of your front sight (the superimposed image should be slightly out of focus with the clearer focus on the front sight.

Sights on most pistols consist of a square front post (with or without a dot), blade or ramp and a rear "U" notch.

- Simply centering the front post in the rear "U" with an even amount of light on both sides of the front post inside the rear notch with their tops level, will give you most of the accuracy you need out to approximately 25 yards (50 with practice).

- In CQB or for shots less than 15 yards perfect sight alignment is often not necessary and tactically may not be advisable (by the time you get a perfect sight picture you adversary may have already closed the gap on you).

- If the front sight is on the target and the rear sight is in close alignment you will hit very close to the front sights position.

- If everyone was expected to maintain a perfect sight picture throughout the trigger squeeze most shooters would never take a shot; however striving for as close to perfect is the ideal.

- Later we will learn how trigger squeeze impacts the shot.

- In CQB/CQC, instinctive or point shooting, many shots are taken based on muscle memory, indexing off of body parts, or off of the muzzle with minimal focus if any on the sights if at all.

Perfect Sight Picture vs. Flash Sight Picture

Perfect Sight Picture – refers to the perfect alignment between the front and rear sights. The further your adversary or target is away, typically the more time you have to secure a perfect sight picture. A perfect sight picture incorporates having the front sight and rear sight perfectly level, and with equal distance on both sides of the front sight in the middle of the rear sights. If you don't jerk the round, the round will typically go pretty close to what you are aimed at. The primary (sharper) focus is still on the front sight with the target or adversary being superimposed behind the front sight.

Flash sight picture – incorporates the quick scanning of an adversary; seeking to first verify the threat (gun, knife, bat, club, ice pick etc); your eyes precede the handgun; your eyes go to the place where you want to hit your target or adversary; it then involves moving your firearm to that spot (bring your gun to your eyes, not your eyes to the gun); and placing at minimum the muzzle on to that point or your front sight preferred and holding it on that spot while you break the round. At this distance the round will typically go pretty close to where you were aimed. The primary (sharper) focus is still on the front sight with the target or adversary being superimposed behind the front sight.

As the weapon recoils you should see the front sight rise and fall. When the front sight returns/drops back down to your desired spot again break the round again and again if necessary until you have neutralized the treat.

One Eye Open or Both Eyes Open

The decision to close one eye or shoot with both eyes open is a matter of preference. Remember a gun fight is nothing more than a fight that involves a gun. If you were having a fist fight with someone you probably would have both eyes open as to maximize your peripheral vision, giving you the widest field of view. In a close quarter firearm encounter you may also want to consider that same logic. When I shoot at close quarters my focus is on the target or adversary. I don't consciously make a decision to close or open one eye.

When I shoot over distance I close the non shooting eye (the eye which is not directly behind the sights). This gives me greater clarity on the sights and helps me assure better sight alignment which is what is required to shoot accurately over distance. If you are a person who has a problem closing one eye then you may want to consider a red-dot or some other type of holographic sight to assist you in aiming your weapon.

Learn to shoot from both sides left and right side. When I shoot with my left hand, I have my left eye open as this allows the eyes, hand, weapon and sights to line up more easily. I do the corresponding thing if my weapon is in my right hand and I make the decision to have only one eye open. Some people have been taught that if the weapon is in the hand of the non-dominant eye, that it is easier to just cock you head to the side or angle your weapon slightly to the side over the dominant eye to enhance alignment (try both and see what works best for you). I however don't subscribe to becoming single or dominant eye focused only. What happens if in the first stages of your close quarter engagement your adversary punches you in your dominant eye or fragments from a near hit land in your dominant eye? I don't think you will have the luxury of calling a time out, so I highly encourage you to learn to utilize both eyes.

BREATHING

At the conclusion of this section you will understand the role breathing plays in pistol shooting, as well as understanding its relationship to rifle shooting. It has been often said that everybody has a fight plan until they get hit! For those who train we hope you will be able to maintain your control. For those who don't train and prepare, after you stop hyper-ventilating the quicker you can control yourself the sooner you can get to the business of handling your business.

- Breathing control is much less important in pistol shooting than in rifle; however it is still important enough to cause a miss, especially at long range (25 yards or more).

- One of the biggest challenges with pistol shooting is we are usually standing up, moving or running while holding a pistol at arms or almost arms length.

- Keep breathing but consider controlled the breaths so that chest movements do not further aggravate the amount of movement already created by the arms.

- Consider taking deep controlled breaths while moving, drawing, getting behind cover etc., and then go to "baby breaths" or shooting at the bottom of the "breath arch," while actually aiming and squeezing the trigger. In a close quarter engagement remember to stay threat and front sight focused; your breathing will probably take care of itself.

TRIGGER SQUEEZE

At the conclusion of this section you will understand multiple types of triggers, and the importance of trigger squeeze and how it impacts shooting accuracy and consistency.

- There is a wide variety of trigger "feels" available today:
  -Double/Single Action
  -Single Action
  -Double Action Only
  -Light Double Action (LDA)
  -Glock "safe action" etc.

Do you know the difference between double action and single action triggers?

- The most difficult to master is probably the traditional double/single action. The transition from the first shot's double action to the remaining shot's single action requires the shooter to learn two different trigger techniques and transition between them after the first shot.

- Single-action trigger (SA) performs the single action of releasing the hammer or striker to discharge the firearm each time the trigger is pulled. SA semi-automatic pistols require the hammer be cocked before the first round is fired (i.e. 1911 model handguns).

- Double Action (DA) performs two functions when pulling the trigger the first is cocking the hammer then releasing it to discharge the firearm. When applied to revolvers the trigger also rotates the cylinder.

- Double Action Only is similar to a DA revolver trigger; however there are no single action capabilities. In a semi-automatic pistol with a traditional hammer, the hammer will return to its de-cocked position after every shot.

- Light Double Action (LDA) – performs the same actions as the standard double action trigger, with the exception of the trigger pull is considerably lighter.

- Glock Safe Action - when a round is chambered, the striker is partially retracted under tension. Pulling the trigger completes the striker cocking and then releases it.

- Preset hammers and strikers apply only to semi-automatic handguns. Upon firing a cartridge or loading the chamber, the hammer or striker will reset in a partially cocked position.

Trigger Squeeze basics

- The key to trigger control is a steady rearward squeeze of the trigger (you often hear people refer to it as pressing the trigger, I have never pressed a trigger in my life, although I have pulled many of them…remember pull does not mean jerk).

- The trigger finger should slip into the trigger guard from its "safety" position on the frame only when you are ready to shoot (otherwise it stays on the trigger guard along the side of the frame).

- Guard against "slapping" the trigger, once you make contact with the trigger.

- (A). Once inside of the trigger guard, the area of the first pad of the forefinger between the center of the pad and first knuckle should touch the trigger (try to shoot off the center of your index fingers fingerprint).

(B). Having the trigger touched down in the crevice of the first joint of the finger will cause the gun to pull to the left or right and slightly down instead of staying exactly where the sights are aligned.

- The trigger squeeze should be a smooth rearward steady motion.

- Watch the front sight and align it with the target while the trigger is being pulled rearward (not jerked). When the trigger breaks should come as a surprise to you.

- You should be able to call your shots by remembering where the front sight was on the target, the moment the trigger broke.

Trigger Practice

- Practice Trigger control by dry-firing your pistol at home.

- Use a target on the wall.

- Make sure the pistol is unloaded (check at least three times, after you have put all ammunition in another room)!

- Then, practice all the earlier points while aiming at your "target."

- Never dry-fire more than 50 times in each session, before taking a break.

- When you feel fatigued take a break to allow you to maintain your concentration and technique (during your break re-read all of your instructions to allow you to correct any mistakes from the earlier session).

- You cannot dry-fire too much!

- Focusing on the front sight and trigger control are the keys to shooting well.

The basics simplified. There is no magic formula for shooting, consistent shooting requires these simple concepts:

1. Sight Alignment – learning to center the front sight in the middle of the rear sight. In close quarter engagements it is remembering to stay front sight focused.

2. Trigger Control – learning to squeeze the trigger and not jerking it. Remember to focus on resetting the trigger, as this allows for quicker more accurate follow up shots.

3. Follow Through – learning to stay on your sights longer as you break the round. Resist the temptation to bring the weapon down quickly to assess your shots. You should see multiple sight pictures on every shot (the one before you break the round and the one after you break the round).

The sooner you incorporate these concepts into your shooting, the sooner you will engrain the fundamentals. There is no such thing as advanced shooting; there is only advanced application of the basics.

Stopping Power & Shot Placement

At the conclusion of this section you will understand the two leading theories on Stopping Power and Shot Placement.

- *Stopping Power – refers to a weapon's or particular cartridge ability to incapacitate an adversary quickly, regardless of whether death ultimately ensues.*

- There are two major schools of thought on the issue:

  1. one group favors the lightweight, high-speed, small-caliber hollow-point bullet of .38/.357/9 mm. Advocates of this philosophy rely on the theoretical expansion of these high-speed bullets in the body of the adversary to create massive physical damage or hydrostatic shock and thereby incapacitation.

  2. The second groups favor the use of large-caliber bullets .44/.45 of comparatively slower velocity. They believe expansion is not required if you begin with a large enough bullet in the first place. The thought is a large bullet will cause more flesh and organ damage.

- There is no exact science when it comes to selection…the best you can do is make an informed, intelligent decision about weapons, calibers and their uses. All are significantly enhanced by your marksmanship capabilities, as that is the most objective way to have a positive ballistic impact on the threat.

- If you feel deadly force is your only option then you should understand these basics. A bullet incapacitates in two ways:

  1. one ways is by causing enough blood loss in the adversary to stop him or her (sometimes referred to as draining the pump).

  2. The second way is damaging the central nervous system (brain or spine). A brain shot is pretty conclusive, the challenge is a clean brain shot is difficult for most people to execute, particularly in a stressful situation (sometimes referred to as turning off the power).

The target zones below will generally address the concern:

- Brain
- Heart
- Lungs
- Spine

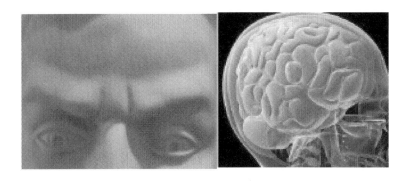

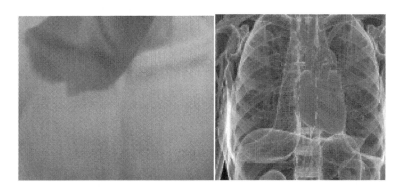

Understanding your Accuracy or Limitations

- To increase the accuracy of your shot placement

- To minimize mis-hits/collateral damage when firing at close or longer ranges.

- To maximize your ability to neutralize a threat.

The grouping process begins by firing three round groups at the below yardages:

Distance	Size of 3 shot group	Manufacturer	Rounds on Target (Y or N)
3 yards			
5 yards			
7 yards			
10 yards			
15 yards			
20 yards			
25 yards			

Continue this process with multiple types of ammunition from multiple manufacturers until you find the optimal load and manufacturer type that best performs in your weapon.

If this handgun is for home defense, it is highly recommend you become familiar with the farthest distance you feel you may engage an adversary in your home. Become familiar with the length of that potential shot to be taken and your accuracy associated with the type of shot, distance and manufacturer of the ammunition you have selected. You should continue to practice that shot until you can consistently defend yourself or your family from that distance. Also since 80% of firearm encounters happen within 7 yards, you may want to concentrate the bulk of your training within those ranges.

MAXIMIZING YOUR HANDGUNS EFFECTIVENESS – ENGAGEMENT ZONES

Green Light Zone

- Typically 0 – 7 yards;
- 80% of most firearm encounters typically occur within 7 yards (50 plus % within 10 feet)!

If you have an encounter with your handgun, there is a good chance it will be up close and personal. Remember at this distance proximity can negate skill. At this distance your instinctive capabilities (muscle memory and your training) are often keys to helping you survive the encounter. Heightened accuracy is typically associated with the operator's ability to index the muzzle, their body parts or just the front sight on the target.

A perfect sight picture at this distance is usually not required and tactically is probably not realistic if your adversary is armed or very well trained in hand to hand skills. Often times at this distance a flash sight picture is all you will have time for.

Yellow Light Zone

- Typically 10 to 25 yards,
- your reaction time may be slightly increased in this zone.

This is where you may still be able to place a quality shot either center mass or to the head. The further you move away from your target or threat, traditionally the advantage goes to the skilled shooter.

This is often the distance where a perfect sight picture may start to be realized to help you accurately execute your shot.

Red Light Zone

- Typically beyond 25 yards (25 – 50 yards),
- this is where the handgun may start to lose a large degree of its effectiveness (unless you train at this distance often).

This is often a distance where you may increase your liability as you may be asked to consider did you have other options available to escape and avoid the potential encounter. The further your potential adversary or threat is away, the more you have to determine or be able to explain why you feel you were at risk? To potentially help increase your accuracy if you are engaging at this distance; you may want to ask yourself is a kneeling or prone position a better shooting platform than a standing one for this distance? This is often the distance where a perfect sight picture may be required to accurately execute your shot.

It is important to practice at multiple distances so that you understand your own limitations. We should also realize in a high stress situation or defensive encounter we will probably only shoot half as good under those conditions as we do on our best day at the range!

Chapter 4

PRESENTING YOUR WEAPON (THE DRAW)

OPEN GARMENT

- The Presentation or Draw from an open garment starts with you in a relaxed standing position.

- The strong side hand goes up to the chest as if saying the pledge of allegiance.

- The strong side thumb works inside the lapel (or you can grab the edge of the lapel) of the cover garment and you wipe down and across toward your holstered weapon.

- At this point your strong side hand grips the handgun high on the grip/back strap; the reaction/support hand simultaneously goes to the center of the chest (at the solar plexus).

- Holstered weapon comes straight up out of the holster muzzle down as high as you can reach naturally than rotates 90 degrees toward the target or adversary and joins the support hand at the center of your chest.

- You are now in a compressed ready position and you can immediately start handling your business from here or anywhere along the line of fire as you thrust your arms forward bringing the weapon up to eye level.

- Stay threat focused and bring the weapon to your eyes (into your sightline) not your eyes to the weapon.

CLOSED GARMENT

- The Presentation or Draw from a closed garment starts with you in a relaxed standing position.

- The reaction/support side hand goes across the body directly to the bottom hem of the cover garment directly above your holster firearm.

- The support side hand has one primary purpose CLEAR THE GARMENT to allow the strong side hand to secure the weapon.

- At this point your strong side hand grips the handgun high on the grip/back strap; the support hand simultaneously goes to the center of the chest (at the solar plexus).

- Holstered weapon comes straight up out of the holster muzzle down as high as you can reach naturally than rotates 90 degrees toward the target or adversary and joins the reaction/support hand at the center of your chest.

- You are now in a compressed ready position and you can immediately start handling your business from here or anywhere along the line of fire as you thrust your arms forward bringing the weapon up to eye level.

- Stay threat focused and bring the weapon to your eyes (into your sightline) not your eyes to the weapon.

THE DRAW SEQUENCE

The sequence should be:

1. Grip – as high up on the grip as you can.

2. Clear – pull your weapon straight up and clear the holster.

3. Rotate – rotate the muzzle 90 degrees toward the target or adversary.

4. Extend – your weapon out toward the target (simultaneously bringing the weapon out and up into your sightline).

Practice Drills to Enhance your Draw

Holster up your gun in your normal carry holster or rig. It is critically important that you practice using the same tools you work in or carry everyday; because in the moment of truth that will probably be the gear you will have on. To beat the street you have to train for the street.

From the holster, without a timer or stop watch, draw your pistol. Your start position should look something the pictures above. Your reaction hand should be to your chest about at your solar plexus:

Drill 1

Do 20 reps of your draw at 1/4 speed – this is designed to familiarize and engrain the basic mechanics for this drill. Each repetition of the draw should be conducted on a mental count, while maintaining fluidity of motion. It should sound something like this – "1Grip, 2 Clear, 3 Rotate, 4 Extend".

Do 20 reps at 1/4 speed

Drill 2

Do 20 reps 1/2 speed

Again, you're looking for consistency and fluidity of motion. This is not a speed drill this is a fluidity of motion drill, designed to remove the kinks.

Drill 3

Do 20 reps at Full speed

At this time your draw should feel considerably faster but not rushed. "Full speed" should be as fast as you can get the gun out of the holster and on target while maintaining control over your body mechanics and a fluid motion on the draw. If you start trying to jerk, cut back on the speed until you can maintain the fluidity of motion. A fast draw time for this is drill is in the 1.5 second range. The purpose of this drill is to build the consistency and economy of motion speed will come.

Consistency + Economy of Motion = Speed

Since the first gunfight shooters have had an ongoing quest for speed. Particularly when it comes to engaging multiple adversaries or in close quarter encounters. You often don't need to learn to shoot faster; you often just need to shoot sooner.

With ongoing practice you will start to become more consistent with your draw. As you enhance the mechanics of your draw you will start to bring your weapon into your sightline sooner, giving you the ability to break the round earlier which will by default make your shots quicker!

Chapter 5

LOADING AND UNLOADING YOUR FIREARM

At the conclusion of this section you will understand the proper techniques to load and unload either revolvers and/or semi-automatic pistols

Loading will be handled in maintaining continuity of fire.

UNLOADING A REVOLVER

- Hold the revolver in your support hand

- Keep the muzzle pointed downrange and/or toward the ground

- Activate the cylinder release with the strong hand thumb

- Once the cylinder is open point the muzzle slightly upward while pushing the ejector rod

- Visually check the cylinder to make sure it is empty

Unloading the Revolver

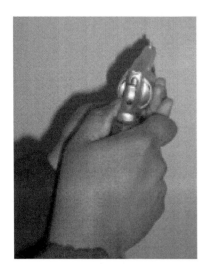

- Hold the weapon in your strong hand

- Keep the muzzle pointed downrange and/or toward the ground

- Finger out of the trigger guard and indexed along the side of frame (below the slide and on or just above the trigger guard)

- Activate the magazine release button with your thumb (while catching the magazine with your support hand)

- Rack the slide (pushing the slide to the rear with your support hand, keeping it clear of the muzzle) then discharge any round which may be in the chamber

- Lock the slide to the rear by activating the slide lock

- Visually check the ejector port to make sure the chamber is empty

- In low light or as a final check you can also place your finger in the ejection port to check for brass

Maintaining Continuity of Fire

At the conclusion of this section you will understand how to load and reload your firearms as well as the importance of maintaining the continuity of fire:

- The major rule of thumb around reloading is "reload when you want to, not when you have to!"

- A gun fight is like a fist fight, you want to hit your adversary as fast as you can as often as you can, until you neutralize the threat.

- There is only one reason to reload, to allow you the ability to maintain the ability to fire.

- To truly maintain continuity of fire requires you to leave one round in the chamber (tactical reload) and discarding the empty or partial magazine (partial magazines should be placed in your pocket vs. discarded, as you may need the partially filled magazine later in the fight) in order to replace it with a fresh magazine.

- Keeping one round in the chamber allows you the ability to take a shot real-time during the reload if required, and eliminates the need to operate the slide release.

ADMINISTRATIVE RELOAD

Administrative Reload is a proactive and preparatory loading procedure and is done in advance of a fire-fight or engagement. It is done under a no stress environment.

- Hold the Handgun in the strong hand or keep it in your holster.

- Keep your finger off the trigger and the muzzle pointed in a safe direction.

- If your weapon is loaded, push the magazine release button with your strong hand thumb and check to make sure the current magazine is at full capacity.

- If it is not at full capacity place the partial magazine in your pocket.

- Stage the flat portion of the magazine against the flat portion of the magazine well.

- Seat it firmly into the magazine well.

- Cycle the action and insert a round into the chamber.

- Safety on or off is a matter of personal preference or duty requirements.

The Revolver

- Hold the weapon in support hand.

- Activate the cylinder release and flip open the cylinder.

- Point your muzzle toward the sky and allow rounds to land into your strong hand. Discard any spent shell casings and refill revolver from your stored ammunition source.

- Close the fully loaded cylinder with the support palm and prepare for or return to duty.

TACTICAL RELOAD (RELOAD WITH RETENTION)

Tactical Reload – is a proactive loading procedure which allows the operator to bring their gun back to desired capacity during the calm in the storm. It is a technique where you maintain control of unused rounds. This is unlike the combat or speed reloads, where you dump remaining live rounds (partial magazines). This may be as the result of the bad guy is down or you have moved to cover during your actual fire-fight and desire to bring your weapon to full capacity in order to continue to handle your business and maintain continuity of fire. The priority in this order should be bringing the gun back to full capacity first, maintaining control of unused rounds second.

Tactical reloading subscribes to the old adage of reload when you want to, not when you have to!

- Hold the Handgun in the strong hand.

- Keep your finger off the trigger and the muzzle pointed in a safe direction or in the direction of the adversary.

- Try to avoid executing a tactical reload while in the kill zone or in the middle of a fire-fight (move to cover).

- Reach for a fresh magazine as you prepare to eject the partially expended magazine.

- Push the magazine release button with your strong hand thumb.

- Catch the partially used magazine between your second and third fingers of your support hand.

- Place the partially used magazine in your pocket vs. in your magazine holder/pouch to allow you to differentiate partial magazines from full ones (full magazines should be kept in your magazine holder/pouch to help you develop consistent ammunition management).

- Stage the flat portion of the new magazine with your support hand index finger riding along side of the magazine up to the top of the first round. When your index finger reaches the bottom of your strong hand pinky (which is wrapped around the firearm) you will know you are at the bottom of the magazine well (this helps you learn to find the magazine well in low light conditions or to keep your eyes on your adversary at all times during the encounter.

- Seat it firmly into the magazine well.

- The support hand then resumes its normal position on the firearm.

The Revolver

- Hold the weapon in support hand.

- Activate the cylinder release and flip open the cylinder.

- Point your muzzle toward the sky and allow the unfired rounds and spent shells to land into your other hand. Take the unfired rounds and place those rounds in your pocket.

- Retrieve a speed loader from your ammunition pouch.

- Properly align the speed loader with your firing hand and insert the rounds halfway into the chamber.

- Release the rounds into the chamber and drop the speed loader.

- Close the fully loaded cylinder with the support palm and return to the action.

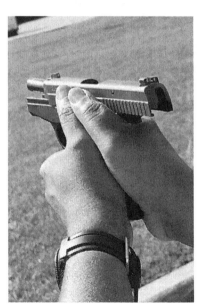

Emergency Reload – is a reactive loading procedure and is done in the middle of a fire-fight or engagement.   It is done under a high-stress environment. It typically comes as the result of a click vs. a bang with a revolver or with a semi-auto weapon the action locks open. *Emergency reloading practice must be conducted from slide-locked, empty gun position.* You want to make the act of releasing the slide and chambering a round instinctive.

- In an unfortunate gun battle the reload will probably come as a surprise when the pistol slide locks back during a fight.

- If you have a back up weapon, it may be quicker to transition to a back up gun (pistol or edged weapon in extreme close quarter situations) if not follow the below instructions.

- Reach for a fresh magazine as you prepare to eject the expended magazine.

- Push the magazine release button with your strong hand thumb.

- Eject the expended magazine as you move to the replacement magazine toward the pistol. Let the spent magazine fall to the ground it is of no use to you when it is empty (remember you are in the middle of a fire-fight).

- Stage the flat portion of the new magazine with your support hand index finger riding along side of the magazine. When your index finger reaches the bottom of your strong hand pinky (which is wrapped around the firearm) you will know you are at the bottom of the magazine well (this helps you learn to find the magazine well in low light conditions or to keep your eyes on your adversary at all times during the encounter.

- Seat it firmly into the magazine well.

- As the support hand resumes its position, release the slide and chamber a fresh round. This allows you to keep your hands on fire control and get and the weapon in your sight line which saves you from having to reacquire the sight picture.

- Some people chose to release the slide by gripping the slide from the back slide serrations and release the slide that way. See below photo. This technique is often very beneficial when wearing gloves, in hot humid weather or when you are concerned about fine motor skills under stress.

The Revolver

Revolver shooters use a different technique, but the concepts remain the same:

- The need to emergency reload will probably be the result of a "click" instead of a "bang."

- Move to cover if possible or try and create distance at a minimum as you reload.

- Bring the pistol off target and open the cylinder with the support hand.

- Pivot the pistol with the muzzle pointing up, punch the ejector rod with the support hand and eject the spent cases.

- At the same time reach for and secure the speed-loader on your belt.

- Place the butt end of the pistol against your belly and stage the speed-loader with the strong hand.

- Activate the release, and discard the empty speed-loader.

- Close the cylinder.

- Get back into the fight.

Chapter 6

MALFUNCTIONS

FAILURES TO FIRE AND MISFIRES FOR SEMI-AUTOS

Failures to Fire or Weapons malfunctions typically fall into one of two categories; either weapons issues or ammunition issues. Weapons issues are often uncontrollable during a fire-fight or tactical engagement. Ammunition problems however may often be addressed during a fire-fight or tactical engagement.

Weapons Failures or Malfunctions are often mechanical problems beyond the shooter's control (i.e. broken firing pin)

Ammunition problems with small arms typically fall into three categories:

Hangfires, Misfires, and Squib Rounds

- Hangfire – refers to an unexpected delay between the triggering of a firearm and in the ignition of a propelling charge. The amount of delay is unpredictable, but in most cases will be a fraction of a second. In some cases, you may not notice the delay. The weapon will function normally.

This failure is often the result of inconsistent quality of the powder or propellant when the cartridge was loaded.

- Misfire – is a complete failure of a propelling charge or primer to function. This may be the result of a bad primer. If a failure to fire (misfire) has occurred take immediate action to eject the cartridge…remember to always keep your weapon pointed in a safe direction (if on the range…the muzzle should be pointed downrange).

- Squib Round – is a round of ammunition with little or no powder charge. This type of round is distinguished by audible pop or reduced recoil. In these cases the shooter should not take immediate action. In the case of a squib round the weapon should not be fired again until the magazine is ejected the chamber is cleared of any rounds and bore of the weapon must be cleared before shooting can continue.

Common Corrective Action Procedures:

Weapon Failure

* Transition to your back up weapon firearm.

* Transition to other tools at your disposal (edged weapon, OC Spray, ASP Baton).

* Consider using your handgun as an impact weapon.

* If you don't have a back up weapon look to execute a tactical escape.

Hangfire

* Keep the weapon pointed in a safe direction (downrange).

* Stay on target or keep the weapon pointed downrange for at least 30 seconds.

* The only time you may want to consider taking immediate action on a hangfire is if you are actually in the middle of a deadly force encounter and you feel getting back in the fight immediately is germane to your safety.

* A hangfire will go off or become a misfire.

Misfire

* Keep the weapon pointed in a safe direction down range.

- Then squeeze the trigger.

- Tap the magazine to ensure it is seated properly.

- Rack the slide.

- Squeeze the trigger.

Squib Round

- Keep the weapon pointed in a safe direction.

- Do not fire the weapon again until it is checked.

  (this should be done my a qualified professional)

- Activate the magazine release and remove the magazine.

- Make sure the chamber is cleared of any rounds.

- The bore of the weapon must be cleared before shooting can continue.

  (this should be done my a qualified professional)

WEAPON NOT FULLY INTO BATTERY

- *Often the result of the magazine not being fully inserted or the result of a round not chambered*

- *Keep the weapon pointed in a safe direction, tap the bottom of the magazine tomake sure it is fully inserted.*

- *Rack the slide.*

- *Squeeze off the next round.*

FAILURE TO EXTRACT (DOUBLE FEED)

- *Upon pressing the trigger nothing happens (no shot discharged). Keep the weapon high and remove your finger off the trigger and place it straight below the slide and along or above the trigger guard. As you look into the ejection port you should notice the brass in the ejection port.*

- *With the reaction/support hand grasp the rear serrations at the back of the slide, then with the strong hand thumb push up on the slide stop to lock the slide to the rear.*

- *Remove the magazine.*

- *Cycle the slide 2 -3 times, to eject any live rounds or empty shell cases.*

- *Once the rounds extracts, insert magazine, chamber a round, and continue firing.*

FAILURE TO EJECT (SMOKE STACK/STOVE PIPE)

- *Upon pressing the trigger nothing happens (no round discharged). Keep the weapon high and remove your finger off the trigger and place it straight below the slide and along or above the trigger guard. As you look into the ejection port you should notice the brass in the ejection port typically sticking straight up on off to the side*

• With the support hand grasp the rear serrations at the back of the slide, then in one motion rotate the weapon to the right (ejection port down) and cycle the slide, this should allow gravity to make the lodged round fall to the ground

• Rotate the weapon back the left so the sights are back on top and you are now back in the fight. Require target and proceed with handling your business

Chapter 7

Engaging the Threat

Dealing with Multiple Adversaries

Dealing with multiple Adversaries

Over 50% of the time we will face more than one adversary. Dealing with multiple adversaries is never at the top of anyone's to do list. Staying alert and avoiding the situation is always the preferred option one.

Below are some tactical considerations for dealing with multiple adversaries:

- If possible try and execute a tactical escape. If a tactical escape is not available you must try and stack the engagement in your favor.
- Try and engage the adversaries from behind cover (cover has ballistic stopping capabilities) or at minimum concealment (concealment can't stop a bullet, but can at least hide you from the threats view…if it is harder to see you it is typically harder to hit you).
- Proactive movement - this may come as surprised counter attack (i.e. you are home and undetected by your adversaries and are able to move to a safe position before launching your

countermeasures).

- Reactive movement – this may occur when you have been detected or singled out and your movement was required to try and improve your defensive or offensive position.

- The first threat you engage should be the one who has the greatest ability to harm or kill you. The ability to harm you is often tied to the adversaries focus not merely weapon type or proximity alone.

The below photos represent your worst case scenario. You have made the decision you are forced to have to engage. You are trying to flank or line your adversaries up, this allows you to get your shots on line faster by reducing the amount of muzzle movement required to hit the next adversary.

The below two photos shows potentially your third or fourth position depending on the reaction of your adversaries. Your goal if possible is to line your shots up to allow faster muzzle transition. Hopefully you have had a positive ballistic impact at minimum on the adversary closest to you (the bad guy in the white shirt). As you notice the adversary on the far right is trying to move outside of his fellow adversary as the bad guy in the white shirt was blocking his initial shot on you. Your goal in this situation would have been to try to continue moving to your left to use the other bad guy as cover as long as you could.

- You should attempt to get a least one shot on or at minimum in the direction of all of the bad guys as opposed to double or triple tapping one bad guys as his friends will probably not stop shooting or trying to harm you during the fight.
- If you are a tactical team or family with multiple armed members you should decide who will engage whom to allow you to be more efficient in dealing with the threat.
  -consider non verbal signals or
  -low whispers

- If as example you are defending in the home and the other family members are not trained allowing the trained family member to handle the business alone may be the best option as the others stay behind cover or attempt to escape if the counter attack was designed to provide suppression fire.

Moving Targets

Once you learn how to develop a good shooting platform there are only four ways to miss a moving target:

- Above
- Below
- Behind
- In front

Once you learn how to move your gun on a horizontal plane, on the same line as the target, or portion of the target you wish to hit, then the only thing we have to do is now work on lead or trail. If the target is moving faster than we are we rely on leading the target (point of aim, is slightly ahead of intended point of impact) in order to hit it. If the target is moving slower than we are, we rely on trailing the target (point of aim, is slightly behind intended impact) in order to hit it.

Reactive or Point Shooting

Reactive shooting like all close quarter engagements involves quick reactions and involves good hand eye coordination or learning to work from body indexing (which may involve little to no sight acquisition). In reactive or point shooting our focus is primarily on the adversary. Learning to watch your adversary or staying alert while searching for your adversary is of critical importance. The effective introduction of your weapon will come as a conditioned response with proper training. Learn to move your weapon to your eyes not your eyes to the weapon, as your eyes are naturally focused on the threat.

Once you learn to establish a good shooting platform, your front sight will become like a third eye, and your subconscious will learn to move the weapon to the threat as your eyes move to or scan the threat. When scanning the target be highly conscious of focusing on the adversary hands prior to scanning the remainder of the body.

ENGAGING THREATS ON THE MOVE

- If the target is moving faster than you, then your point of aim will be slightly ahead of your intended point of impact; your adversary will move into your shot.

- If you are moving faster than the target, then your point of aim will be slightly behind your intended point of impact; you will move the shot into the adversary.

- If the threat is moving directly toward you or directly away from you, you can align you shot directly at the treat without leading or trailing the shot.

- When dealing with multiple threats and moving your muzzle between them you must learn to move your muzzle on the recoil as you line up your next shot to be taken.

- Allow your eyes to move to where the adversaries are, bringing your weapon to your eyes. The goal is to learn to move your upper body like a tank turret so where your eyes go the muzzle instinctively points. This allows you to break your next shot faster.

- When you are moving try to keep your feet moving in the direction you are heading this allows for greater control, and gives you a wider range of motion increasing your turn radius.

Allow your upper body to square to the target and learn to keep your knees slightly flexed (this will help stabilize your platform) to help maintain body control and enhance the accuracy of your shots.

FIGHTING IN AND AROUND YOUR HOUSE

Fighting in and around your house can take on many forms depending on your objective. Clarity of objective and the subsequent tactical execution is essential to helping you survive the encounter.

Below are some of the more common tactical approaches one may consider:

Holding your Position - this is the most common home defense scenario. Despite the initial anxiety, remember time and the element of surprise is on your side (*it is your house* or pre-established location and *you have a plan*). You have no immediate need to engage your adversary and no reason to search for them; you actually let them come to you! You have established a position of dominance or situational advantage, effectively making use of cover and concealment. You point your muzzle at the predetermined approach area and wait to ambush your adversary. You may or may not choose to warn your adversary; that decision may be dependent on the tactical situation, your defense capabilities and/or legal considerations.

Taking Ground - this involves attacking your attackers. An example may be the rescue of family members about to be victimized. This is similar to a hostage rescue. This involves moving rapidly and/or stealthily to close on your adversaries and neutralize the threat through the use of precision close range gunfire. The urgency of the situation may negate your decision to negotiate, try to de-escalate or give your adversary advanced warning. In this scenario you typically look to locate your adversary, close the gap and place a precision shot on the threat to save innocent victims.

In some cases this may also take the form of seizing a building, room or piece of land to be used to hold a position until help arrives or you are able to execute a tactical escape.

Tactical Escape – this involves traveling through a potential conflict area where there may be hostiles. The objective is not to engage, but rather to escape. You and your protectees may move rapidly or slowly through and out of the threat area. There is no time to clear or search. As you execute your escape you allow your muzzle to cover any areas of danger slicing the pie as appropriate. The goal is to escape...but in a strong and controlled manner. Remember a tactical escape beats a tactical encounter every time!

Search and Clear - this is probably the least desirable of all the options, as it is basically a hunt for the bad guy. This is the scenario most replicated in police or military "shoot-house" room clearing training, and should only be executed by trained professionals or a last option. This involves you moving cautiously and deliberately through an area in search for an adversary. That adversary may be hidden (prepared to fight or not) or totally unaware your presence.

Regardless of the particular strategy you decide to employ they; all will require an understanding of the architectural features of the building involved, the appropriate tactics and how to negotiate them, the cadence of your movements, the ability to identify danger areas and potential threats, and the ability to adopt diverse fighting platforms consistent with situation and the environment.

Whether you are operating alone, with your family, a partner, or as a member of a team you will need to be clear on your objective and tactics.

Keys to Surviving a Fire-Fight or Tactical Engagement

Alertness + Anticipation + Distance + Time = Enhances Survival

The ability to stay alert and anticipate situations often gives us the ability to; create distance; which buys us more time; which increases our ability to execute a tactical escape or place a better quality shot; both of which significantly enhance our ability to survive an encounter.

Effective Utilization of Cover

What is the difference between cover and concealment? Cover - has ballistic stopping capabilities (i.e. brick wall, engine block, very large tree etc.). Concealment - can't stop a bullet, but can at least hide you from the threats view…if it is harder to see you it is typically harder to hit you (i.e. drywall, sofa, outside hedges, car door etc).

Keys to using cover or concealment:

- Try to stay at least 4 -6 feet back from your cover:
  -this will allow any ricochets to potentially go around or over you and not into you
  -this will also reduce the possibilities of any shattered debris from possibly injuring you

- Allow your shooting platform to match your cover

PRONE POSITION FROM COVER

If all you have is a 2 - 3 foot high fallen log, large rock or automobile wheel well (stay closer to the brake drum) to hide behind, consider a prone position as your firing platform.

- Keep the gun pointed toward the target or adversary.

- Drop down on both knees or one knee at a time if you have

bad knees (the cadence of the fight will help dictate your sense of urgency). While extending your body toward to target or adversary, use your support or reaction side hand to help balance your body, easing down to the ground.

- Extend arms toward the target or adversary and handle your business.

- Pistol may rest on the ground (anytime you employ a rest you typically help minimize recoil) or may be held above the ground.

Advantages

- This is the most stable shooting platform in your arsenal.

- Helps increase accuracy particularly over longer distances.

- This helps make you a smaller target.

- For those wearing body armor helps place more of your body behind the armors protective capabilities.

Disadvantages

- Puts you in a compromising position particularly for attacks from the rear.

- For those lacking flexibility it may make your ability to move to an alternate position tougher.

KNEELING POSITION FROM COVER

If all you have is a 3 – 4 foot high brick wall, large rock or engine block to hide behind you may want to consider a kneeling position as your firing platform.

- *The initial move starts out from the standing position with your eyes and weapon focused on the adversary. Take a step out with the support leg toward the target. Make sure your weapon is already out of the hostler and pointed toward the target or adversary.*

- *Drop down on the strong (holster) side knee.*

- *Extend handgun out toward the target. Try to make your upper body position resemble that of your standing position. You may take a bladed position with your upper body or a parallel position. Proceed to handle your business.*

Advantages

- This is the second most stable platform outside of the prone position.

- Lower body acts as a brace and aids in stabilizing your platform.

- Allows you to make more accurate shots particularly over distances.

- Allows for a stable platform but still allows for ease of movement in the event you need to change positions or locations.

- Helps lower your profile, thereby making you a smaller target.

Disadvantages

- For those with limited flexibility or dexterity, it may make transitioning to other positions or locations tougher.

Optional Kneeling

- Some people prefer to sit down/back on the strong side heel.

- If so keep wait shifted slightly toward the target or adversary.

- Leaning back on the heel can magnify recoil of the firearm.

- Avoid placing your support elbow directly on your knee.

- Avoid bone on bone
  -Place your tricep on your knee or
  -Place your elbow on your quadriceps

- This position is not highly recommended for close quarter engagements as resting your weight on your heel may limit some people's ability to move quickly.

STANDING POSITION FROM COVER

If all you have a very solid vertical structure, tree or door to cover or conceal you, you may want to consider a standing position as your firing platform. Make sure your body position matches the cover (i.e. should I turn sideways).

Cover and or movement are often the two major keys to surviving an attack. There is some truth to the old adage a moving target is harder to hit. Numerous law enforcement and civilian encounters as well as force or force training have shown that people who move off the line of attack, significantly increase their ability to survive a firearm or edged weapon encounter.

KEYS TO USING MOVEMENT (particularly in close quarters)

During an actual attack

- Get off the line of attack.

- People tend to engage you where you were, not where you are now!

- If you cannot move after your first shot, try to at least move after the conclusion of the first encounter.

- Like a boxer your ability to bob or weave is crucial our movement in relation to the face of a clock is our version of bobbing and weaving. Often you can't move totally out of the ring, but you can move off of the line of attack.

- Consider moving to 9, 10, 11, 1, 2, 3, 8, 7, 5, or 4 o'clock.

- Avoid moving straight back to 6 o'clock (unless you are a professional NFL cornerback must people can't move straight back very fast), most bad guys can run forward faster than you can run backwards. It is too easy to get over run or taken down and if your threat has a firearm, and you move straight back, you have not moved out of his or her sight picture!

During a Dynamic Entry or Exit

- Try to alter your standard shooting platform as little as possible.

- The muzzle is typically below eye level to allow you to see over the muzzle.

- If moving with a team in a line, the weapon will typically be in a low ready or Suhl position to minimize covering a team member with your weapon.

- Keep your walking gate as consistent as possible:
  -if you need to close the gap quicker take longer strides
  -if you need to slow down closing the gap, take shorter steps.

- Consider bending your knees a little more and incorporate a slight forward lean to aid in absorbing recoil.

- Remember in a dynamic entry or exit, you cannot move any faster, than your ability to deliver quality hits on your adversary.

- When moving through a fatal funnel (open doorway) or intersection that you must move by or though:

-you must do it with a sense of urgency

-try to move to cover or at minimum concealment as you break the threshold of the door or intersection.

Low Ready   **Sul**

SEARCHING FOR AN INTRUDER

- Always use a trained partner if and when available.
- Wear body armor if available.
- Utilize or be conscious of cover.
- Do not turn your back on un-cleared areas.
- Practice good light discipline.
- Practice safe weapons handling.
- Use ear pieces to silence radios.
- Keep radio traffic to a minimum.
- Move quietly and cautiously.
- Communicate your observations to your partner.
- Cover each other when clearing dark areas and doors.

SLICING THE PIE (CORNERING TECHNIQUES)

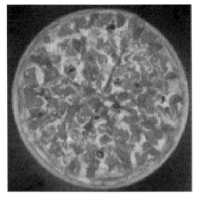 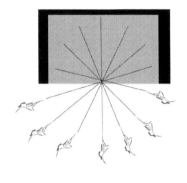

While most building and rooms may vary; the basic clearing techniques however are pretty standard. Clearing a room or corner is like eating a pie and best done one bite at a time:

- Try to maintain the element of surprise.

- Maintain your noise discipline.

- Move slowly.

- One slice at a time.

- In small bites look vertically as well as horizontally.

- Use cover and concealment whenever possible.

- Remember to try and stay 4 – 5 feet off of cover (bullets often ricochet along the surface of your cover).

The above photos represent two different scenarios of what might be waiting for you around the corner. In the first photo we don't know if the bad guy has a weapon or not, but slicing the pie and staying wide allowed us to be able to see the corner of his shoulder.

In the second photo the bad guy makes another mistake in exposing his weapon beyond the cover. Just because they are criminals, it doesn't make them tactically smart. Make sure your muzzle does not extend beyond the cover and compromise your position as you take a corner.

The below photos are designed to help illustrate the "slicing the pie" technique.

Clearing or searches which involve stairs can be extremely dangerous as they force you to expose portions of your body without the ability to lead with your Handgun (leading with your handgun does not mean exposing it prematurely beyond a wall or other structure). When forced to consider clearing steps or escalators make sure that is truly your only option. If you then decide the search must go on; then clear the visible portions that allow you to lead with your Handgun utilizing the slicing the pie techniques. Consider separating the steps or escalator into upper and lower to minimize your exposure.

CONFRONTING AN INTRUDER

- Try to confront an intruder from behind cover.

- Maintain maximum distance and get verbal compliance before approaching.

- Be alert for a possible second intruder.

- Watch the hands for suspected weapons.

- Have the suspect interlock their fingers behind their head.

- Have suspect go to the kneeling position and cross their ankles.

- If necessary have the suspect go to a prone position with arms extended and hands pointing up.

- If the people confronting the intruder or threat are law enforcement or security, one partner covers while the other cuffs the suspect.

- Always cuff before searching.

- Communicate your status to the response team.

Perpetrator/Intruder Down

The stress and adrenaline dump of a deadly force encouter are challenging enough in and of themselves; however, post deadly force encounter the steps you take next are as important as the preparation which allowed to survive the encounter.

in most states you cannot use any more force than the force being used against you and when that force stops so must yours. If you have made the decision to use deadly force you must have felt your life, or that of a family member or a third party was in serious danger. That decision will be sorted out by the judge not me but until then here are some important considerations:

- When the perpetrator is no longer a threat stop shooting.

- While you call the authorities continue to check your surroundings particularly behind you to make sure he has no bad guy buddies trying to sneak up on you.

- Since there is a temporary lull in the storm, take the time to tactically reload your weapon and bring it back to full capacity, just in case the situation further deteriorates.

- Call 911 or ask someone to call the authorities immediately, and ask the dispatcher to send the police. If a family member, client, team m ember, innocent bystander or perpreatrator has been injured also notify them to send an ambulance also (even if you believe the perpetrtor may be fatally injured ask them to send an ambulance anyway). Give the dispatcher a good description of yourself so police may recognize you.

- Now call your attorney. First call is to 911, second call is to your attorney!

- Don't misrepresent the facts (to either the dispatcher or police) or alter evidence at the scene. If you alter evidence eventually it will be found out and your credibility will be lost at that point.

- Secure the weapon. If the perpetrator has a weapon, try and secure the wepaon, this does not necessarily mean picking it up. You may accomplish this by merely instructing the perpetrator to mvoe away from the weapon. There may be times when you may have to literally secure the weapon (for your own safety or the safety of others), if this is the case and you must pick it up, consider sticking an ink pen in the muzzle/barrel and picking it up. Other times you may secure the weapon by slightly moving it away from the perpetators grasp with your foot.

- If you are providing executive protection, have one of the other agents get your client out of harm's away as you remain for the police.

- If a crow appears and they start to become riotous and you no longer feel safe and you must flea, immediately tell the dispatcher if they are still on the line or redial the police as you head straight to the police station.

- As soon as it is tactically possible secure your own weapon in your holster (however holstering your own weapon does not mean not keeping it at the ready). You don't want to be standing there with a gun in your hand when the police arrive. There will be times that you may have to hold a prepetrator at bay, until the police arrive. If that is the case and they say put your gun down. Please heed that advice, you don't want to become an accidental shooting because they thought you were the perpetrator!

- There is a good chance you will at minimum be handcuffed or arrested even in a self-defense shooting, until the police can sort out the situation.

  Remember the police are also concerned for their own safety and since one person is already down, they don't want the second person down to be them.

- Tell the police you would like to press charges or file a complaint against the perpetrator. Point out any witnesses on the scene or relevant evidence the police should be aware of.

- Don't talk to anyone about the case until it has been adjudicated. If you are arrested and placed in a holding cell, avoid talking to anyone about your situation. You never know who may be trying to cut their own deal. Don't talk to your family, friends, co-workers or strangers about the case. People will try and press you for details. Just advise them, "unfortunately this is still an ongoing investigation and I am not at liberty to make any comments." While you may not be charged criminally in the case, it doesn't mean you may not become the party of a civil suit.

WEAPON RETENTION

The primary rule in weapon retention is to stay alert. Keeping an adversary away from your weapon is the first rule of weapon retention. People always want to ask "what do I do once someone grabs my gun?" The major focus needs to be how I get people away from my gun first. Awareness is often the key to not becoming a victim. It is important to understand that your gun may not be the only thing the attacker is looking to take from you.

Key considerations in weapons retention:

- Awareness is always our first defense. Be aware of who is around you.

- If someone grabs for your handgun you need to be aware that they may be prepared to kill you. You must be prepared react immediately.

- If you believe their intent may be the worst case scenario (deadly force situation), you must be more motivated than they are to protect your weapon and most importantly your life.

- Your options are many but most importantly you must be committed to the fight!

- Below are some self-defense basics:
  1. Disrupt their Vision - Attack the eyes
  2. Disrupt their Breathing - Attack the throat
  3. Disrupt their Balance - Attack the groin, quads, knees, chins etc.

Countermeasures

- If someone grabs the muzzle of your Handgun, avoid getting into a tug of war. Simply get the muzzle back on them, and discharge your weapon.

- This often may be achieved while standing by dropping to a knee and firing your weapon the bad guy will probably let go!

- If the bad guy happens to take your weapon and you carry an alternative weapon (handgun or knife), transition to your alternate weapon and handle your business.

- If you don't have an alternate weapon employ your specific close quarter countermeasures (hands, fists, elbows, knees, impact flashlight, ASP baton, pepper spray etc.), you must attack the attacker, remember you need to be more motivated than them at this point to protect your life.

- For some you may feel not fighting back is your best option (although many studies involving police show that when their weapon is taken, they are generally shot with it).

 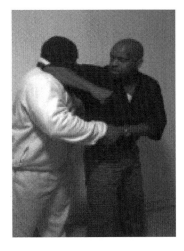

- If someone grabs your weapon simultaneously look to secure your weapon with one hand and strike with the other (you must respond quickly).

- Your elbow is one of the strongest bones in your body and a well placed elbow (chop, fingers to the eyes, palm heel to the face etc.) will often change the channel of your attacker.

- The elbow to the face, neck, ribs, solar plexus, or throat is typically very effective.

- That technique works well for attackers coming from either the front or the back.

- *Secure the attacker's hand with your strong-side hand.*

- *Placing your thumb into the webbing of the attackers hand (the space in between the thumb and your index finger) and grab the meaty part of his hand with your fingers, this will help you maintain a strong grip as you rotate away from the attacker.*

- *Rotating your hips aggressively to the rear and away from your adversary. Often time the aggressive move of the hips in and of themselves will often dislodge the attacker's hand.*

- Learn to separate your tools.

- If you wear your handgun on your right side learn to wear your edged weapons, ASP baton, impact flashlight, OC spray etc. on the opposite side. This will help you if someone is attacking your strong (weapon) side this gives you the ability to transition to alternate tools.

- It is also beneficial if you are being attacked by an additional adversary.

Non-shootable Threat

Just because you have a weapon, all situations don't necessarily call for discharging your weapon. For non-shootable adversaries the Handgun may be used as an impact weapon. *If your weapon is to be used as an impact weapon, your finger must be outside of the trigger guard to avoid an accidental discharge.*

Muzzle Thrust

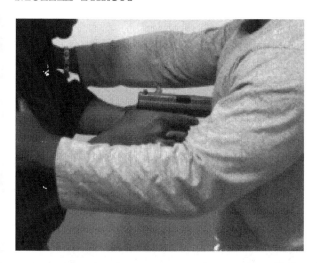

- While holding the Handgun (strong hand on the Handgun wrist, finger out of the trigger guard and indexed along side the trigger guard, the support hand on the forearm) thrust the muzzle of the Handgun into:

-Solar plexus

-Groin

-Chin or face

• Make sure you step into the move…avoid an arms only thrust.

Butt Thrust

- If the adversary is coming toward you step off the line of attack and with your support hand push the adversary away from you (matador move) as you try and step behind them.

- Remember your finger must be off the trigger and along the slide or trigger guard and strike your adversary to the back of the head or neck.

- Make sure you step into the move…avoid an arms only thrust.

High Slide Thrust

- An alternate move on the Butt Thrust but involves aggressively striking the top of the slide anywhere between your adversary's jaw line and neck.

- You may also use the front sight in a striking and pulling moment in and attempt to cause an open wound.

- Make sure you step into the move…avoid an arms only thrust.

Chapter 8

DEALING WITH WHAT GOES
BUMP IN THE NIGHT

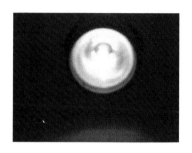 

Keep in mind that over 70% of encounters will occur at night
or in low light conditions. Most criminals prefer night as they
feel they have a greater opportunity to move in the cover of
darkness and potentially avoid detection. In low light conditions
it is important to remain calm. Your movements are often slow
and methodical unless executing a rapid/dynamic entry or exit
maneuver. Often when one sense is taken away the other senses
become heightened. Allow those senses to work for you as you
plan your search or exit.

Be conscious of:

• Noise to help you locate a threat or potential adversary.

- Smell to use your nose to help you detect a potential threat or adversary.

  -body odor

  -cologne or perfume

  -smoke cigarette or tobacco

  -any smells uncommon to your environment

It is often more beneficial to stay put and behind cover let your adversary come to you if an immediate escape is not available to you. *The major reason for a light is not to see the sights on your Handgun, but to identify a potential adversary and provide you positive target acquisition.* This allows you to better scan the environment and when a potential threat is located better scan their body or bodies for potential weapons or monitor their movements.

The light sources may often be standard white, halogen, green or strobe lights. Strobe lights often make it harder for a threat or adversary to pin down your particular position within the illuminated area. Those same lights may also make it harder for you to detect minor movements on a potential adversary.

Please keep in mind once you illuminate an area your position will be compromised. Some considerations when utilizing a light:

- In defensive or tactical situations you should avoid using a light unless or until absolutely necessary.

- Consider using short bursts of lights 1 – 2 seconds on then off as you scan and area, if no threat is detected, with the light off move to a new location before turning it on again.

- Move low and slow.

- Angle the beam of light at the ceiling as this allows the light to reflect off the ceiling and illuminate more of the room.

- If working with a team member or family member, keep a little distance between yourselves; making it harder for the adversary to line you up.

- If a potential threat is detected, remember scan the body with particular focus on hands and feet as they have the ability to be used most quickly in a threatening or harmful manner.

- If your partner says moves outside of the light beam he or she will often remain almost invisible to the potential threat.

- The person holding the light should keep it pointed in the direction of the potential threat but both that person and the other team or family member also should remain alert to other sounds or possible movements as the potential threat may not be alone. Remember to be conscious of what is potentially behind you (check your six).

LIGHT FIGHTING POSITIONS

There are a multitude of light opens you can consider. They range from integrated operating systems (light attached to your weapon); to the simplest option of holding a traditional hand held light in your support hand. They may be operated by on/off buttons mounted on the side or rear of the light source to pressure switches.

INTEGRATED HANDGUN LIGHT

- Integrated lights allow you to grip your handgun in your normal position.

- The light may be operated by an on/off switch in the back of the light or may be operated by a pressure switch.

Backhand (Harries) Position

- Works like the Weaver shooting position.

- While gripping the flashlight in a backhand fist, the gun hand comes forward and creates dynamic tension as it presses against back of the flashlight hand.

- The flashlight arm pulls toward the body similar to the Weaver stance.

- Heavy or longer flashlights may be rested on the strong hand's forearm to help reduce fatigue during extended use.

Thumbs Forward (Chapman) Position

- The thumb and forefinger of the support hand hold the light.
- The thumb of the support hand points forward toward the target or adversary.
- The remaining fingers wrap around the gun hand for a two hand grip.
- This techniques works well for flashlights with side-mounted switches.
- The disadvantage of this technique typically comes into play with operators with small hands using a heavy flashlight.

FBI Modified

- The Modified FBI technique is accomplished by holding the flashlight in an "ice pick" grip with the arm extended away from the body and the gun hand.

- The hands-apart technique helps the operator avoid "marking" their position through intermittent use of light at random heights.

- The technique also works well with right or left hand shooting.

- The light is often held a multiple heights to avoid identifying the operator's center of mass.

- To prevent the user from self-illumination, the flashlight is held slightly in forward of the body.

- The major disadvantage of this technique is operator may become fatigued during extended use. It also requires extensive practice to perfect as most people are not use to making both hands operate simultaneously, but independently performing fine motor skills.

- The Neck-Index technique is achieved by holding the flashlight in an "ice pick" grip against the jaw/neck line below the ear.

- This allows the light to move with the operator's head with minimal impact on the operator's peripheral vision.

- For larger flashlights, the body of the flashlight can be rested on the shoulder and indexed against the base of the neck.

- Finger activation is dependent on the type of flashlight, either the thumb (tailcap pushbutton) or another finger (side-mounted switch) operates the switch.

- The disadvantage of this position is it may draw fire directly at the operators head.

ROGERS/SUREFIRE (SYRINGE TECHNIQUE)

- The flashlight is held between the forefinger and middle finger of the non-firing hand with the tailcap pushbutton positioned against the palm/base of thumb (similar to how a Doctor or Nurse would grip a syringe).

- The flashlight (reaction) hand is then brought together with the strong hand, the two unused fingers of the reaction hand wrap around the gripping fingers of the strong hand below the trigger guard as normal to form a two hand firing grip.

- The light is activated by exerting pressure to depress the tailcap pushbutton.

In low light situations the potential threat or adversary has four major options:

- Stay hidden if they have not been detected.

- Choose to fight.

- Choose to flee.

- Choose to comply with your commands.

Please be very conscious that once you light an area you have compromised your position. Since the threat now realizes you are there and may consider any of the above once you turn the light off to move again. You need to remain mentally and physically prepared to deal with any of the above options.

Below are some of the more popular used Handgun light and laser companies:

- Crimson Trace
- Insight Technologies
- LaserMax
- Surefire
- Streamlight

Chapter 9

ONE HAND OPERATION

Mike Tyson once said everybody has a fight plan until they get hit. While very admirable we would love to think because of our superior training we will never be injured during an encounter. For those who are veterans of multiple encounters, the reality is there is a good chance we may be injured or at minimum be forced to use our other hand for other activities (i.e. moving another person out of the way, carrying something or someone). While we may not be injured we may be forced to cover an intruder with one hand as we dial the police with the other one.

The most difficult challenge in manipulating your handgun with one hand will typically be the weight of the weapon or maintaining stability. However in a real fire-fight your adrenaline, willingness to survive or protect your family will probably give you the added strength, to perform the operations, but you will still need the technique and training to execute them.

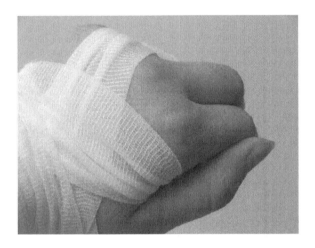

One Hand Stances

- *One of the quickest and most efficient one hand stances is to imagine you are a boxer and stand with your weapon foot forward, hands resembling a boxer's defensive position.*

- *Now image you are throwing a quick straight right hand punch (clinch your left hand and hold it close to your chest).*

- *Now repeat this position with your weapon in your forward hand, out over your strong side leg, left fist is clinched and held close to your chest (this helps tighten up the chest muscles and aids in managing recoil and enhances stability).*

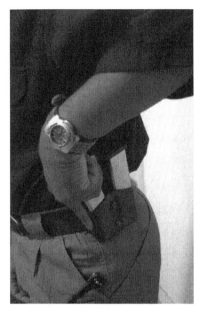

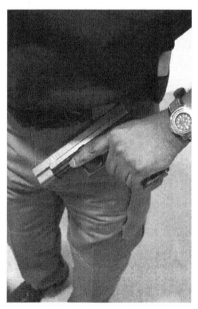

LOADING THE SEMI-AUTOMATIC HANDGUN:

Loading the semi-automatic handgun:

- Try to work from cover if possible or at minimum try to create distance until you can get back into the fight.

- Hit the magazine release button and discard the used magazine.

- Place the Handgun between your knees.

- The Front sight pointing down/magazine well point out.

- Muzzle pointed toward the ground.

- Grab a new magazine and insert it into the magazine well with your non injured arm/hand.

- Rack the slide by placing your rear sight against your belt loop, belt buckle, holster, magazine carrier or boot heel.

- Eyes remained focused on the threat or adversary.

Two different options for one hand or injured operator reloading:

- Placing the handgun between your knees.

- The potential disadvantage of between your knees is if you are startled you may move or run off dropping your weapon.

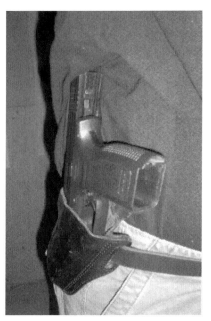

- Placing the hadngun backwards in your holster.

Alternate Technique

- From an Emergency or Tactical Reload position drop down to a kneeling position.

  (be careful when assuming this position so the muzzle doesn't cover your body when loading the magazine or returning to fire control)

- Place the weapon in the crease of the down knee.

- Up knee and foot is forward to avoid being covered by the muzzle.

Handling your Business

- Now it is time to get back in fight.

- Remember you may fire from a standing, kneeling or prone position.

- The most important thing is to stay in the fight if a tactical escape has not presented itself to you.

- Throughout the engagement your eyes have stayed focused on the threat or adversary.

- You may have incorporated your belt, or tee-shirt to make an impromptu sling if required.

CYCLING THE ACTION (RACKING THE SLIDE)

Racking the Slide Off Your Belt Buckle

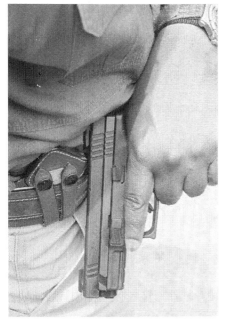

Racking The Slide Off Your Holster

Racking the Slide Off Your Magazine Carrier

Racking The Slide Off Your Heel

Alternate Tactic for Injured Operators (Weapon Transition)

Some considerations for transitioning to an alternate weapon when and if:

- The handgun is damaged.

- The handgun is too heavy for you to manage with one hand.

- You are out of or extremely low on handgun ammunition.

- You are about to get into an extreme close quarter engagement.

- Transition to your impact flashlight, edged weapon, OC spray, ASP Baton etc.

- Throughout the engagement your eyes stay focused on the threat or adversary.

The above picture shows a transition to OC spray.

Appendix

Frequently Used Firearm Terms

Accuracy – the measure of precision in consistently obtaining a desired result. In shooting, the measure of a bullet's or gun's precision in grouping all shots close to the center of impact.

Action – the mechanism of a firearm by which it is loaded, locked, fired and unloaded. In a revolver, usually means the cylinder. In semi-automatic Handguns it usually refers to the slide. In rifles, refers to the bolt mechanism.

Automatic Weapon – a firearm is said to be an "automatic weapon" if it is capable of firing more than one cartridge by pressing the trigger.

Barrel – the part of a firearm the bullet passes through before exiting the firearm.

Bench rest – a heavy table or shelf, which a Handgun or rifle can be fired.

Bore – the inside of the barrel of a gun of any kind.

Bullet – The missile only, becomes a projectile when in flight. Not to be applied to the cartridge.

Caliber – approximately bore or grove diameter expressed (in English) in decimals of an inch, otherwise in the metric system.

Cartridge – a complete unit of ammunition assembled (i.e. case, propellant powder, primer and bullet or shot). Usually only applied to rifle and handgun ammunition, but occasionally to Handgun shotshells.

Center Fire (CF) – refers to centrally located primer in the base metallic cartridges. Most center fire cartridges are reloadable.

Chamber – the part of the bore at the breech, formed to accept and support the cartridge, shell or slug

Clip – a metal device that holds a number of cartridges for fast loading into the magazine of a rifle or Handgun.

Firearm – generally a "gun" carried and used by one person.

FPS – abbreviation for feet-per-second. Also ft/se, fps or f.p.s.

Grooves – spiral cuts or impressions in the bore of a firearm which cause a bullet to spin as it moves through the barrel.

Group – the pattern made at the target of number of shots fired with one aiming point and usually one sight setting. Usually measured from center to center of the holes farthest from each other.

Magazine – that portion of a firearm which holds the cartridges in preparation for the bolt, slide or mechanism to feed a cartridge from the magazine into the chamber. Magazines may be fixed as an internal portion of the firearm or removable. They may be square, tubular or round/drum like.

Misfire – complete failure of a cartridge to fire after the primer is struck by the firing pin.

Muzzle – the front end of the barrel. The point at which a projectile or shot leaves the barrel.

Primer – also called "cap," deriving from "percussion cap" which is the priming form used with some muzzle loading arms.

Projectile – a bullet or any other object projected by force and continuing in motion by its own inertia. A bullet is not a projectile until it is in motion.

Recoil – the backward thrust or "kick," of a gun caused by the reaction to the powder gases pushing the bullet or shot shell through the bore and jet effect of the gasses themselves.

Rifling – parallel spiral grooves cut or impressed into the bore of rifles and Handguns in order to make the bullets spin, insuring steady, and point on flight to the target.

Round – a military term meaning one complete cartridge.

Semi-automatic – a firearm that fires one cartridge (and only one cartridge) each time the trigger is pressed. Semi-Automatic firearms eject the empty cartridge, load a fresh cartridge from the magazine, chamber the cartridge and lock the breech automatically.

Sighting In – firing of a weapon to determine its point of impact at a specified range and to adjust the sights so the point of impact matches the sights.

Velocity – the speed at which a projectile travels, it is usually measured in feet per second (fps) at a given range.

Zero – that adjustment of a gun's sight that will place an aimed shot at the desired point of impact at a given range.

Your Name

Score:

Instructions - Please circle the correct answer:
True or False

1. Below are the top 6 reason consumers purchase firearms?
    True or False

    -Recreational Shooting
    -Competitive Shooting
    -Duty
    -Hunting
    -Collecting
    -Personal Protection

2. We should all understand when we discharge our firearms; we are responsible for those rounds until they stop (and even after that). That is why constant training, care and discretion should be used whenever we take a shot? True or False

3. 80% of gunfights occur within the 7 yard distance? True or False

4. 40% of gunfights occur outside of 25 yards? True or False

5. Hollow point bullets are often used for personal protection or to reduce over-penetration? True or False

6. Polymer insert bullets are designed to prevent the hollow-point cavity from being clogged with fibers and other materials, which can inhibit reliable bullet expansion (i.e. Corbon Powerball, Hornady Critical Defense)? True or False

7. Full Metal Jacket Bullets are often referred to as hardball; and often used by the military based on their design to minimize expansion or deformation? True or False

8. Hot Range – is range where guns are expected to be loaded all the time without commands to reload by the range officer? True or False

9. Safe Zone – is everywhere behind the line of fire. This is where you want to keep all of your body parts. You should avoid having your weapon un-holstered or pointed in the safe zone. True or False

10. Both Administrative and Tactical Reloads are proactive ammunition management techniques? True or False

11. Emergency Reload or is a reactive ammunition management technique? True or False

12. Slicing the pie is a room clearing technique where the operators searches or clears a room in small segments at a time? True or False

13. A key consideration when using cover is allowing our shooting platform to match the cover available? True or False

14. The major reason for a light on Handgun is to see the front sights? True or False

15. In order to hit a moving target which is moving faster than you it is important to trail the target? True or False

16. The major difference between cover and concealment is one has ballistic stopping capabilities and one doesn't? True or False

Multiple Choice Questions - Please circle the correct answer:

17. Which of the below is not one of the cardinal rules of firearm safety?

a) Treat all guns as if they are always loaded.

b) Never point the muzzle at anything you aren't willing to destroy.

c) Keep your finger on the trigger at all times.

d) Watch what is in the background of your target in case you miss.

18. Which of the following is not a component of a semi-auto pistol?

   a) Hammer
   b) Slide
   c) Cylinder
   d) Magazine Release
   e) Slide Lock

19. Which of the following is not a component of a revolver?

   a) Hammer
   b) Front Sight
   c) Cylinder
   d) Ejector Rod
   e) Magazine Release

20. Which of the following are components of a cartridge?

   a) Bullet
   b) Cartridge Case
   c) Gunpowder
   d) Primer
   e) All of the above

21. Which of the below are things you may want to consider when purchasing a holster?
    a) Will this be used for business or personal use
    b) Body type
    c) Lifestyle
    d) Retention requirements
    e) All of the above

22. Which of the following should be followed when unloading a revolver?
    a) Hold the revolver in your support hand
    b) Keep the muzzle pointed downrange and/or toward the ground
    c) Activate the cylinder release
    d) Once the cylinder is open point the muzzle slightly upward while pushing the ejector rod
    e) Rotate the muzzle back down and visually check the cylinder to make sure it is empty
    f) All of the above

23. Which of the following should be followed when unloading a semi-auto?
    a) Hold the pistol in your strong hand (with the trigger finger indexed along the slightly below the slide and along the top of the trigger guard)
    b) Keep the muzzle pointed downrange and/or toward the ground
    c) Activate the magazine release button with your thumb (while catching the magazine)

d) Rack the slide (pushing it to the rear with your support hand…be sure the support hand stays clear of the muzzle… strong hand trigger finger is outside of the trigger guard) dislodge any round which may be in the chamber

e) Visually check the ejector port to make sure the chamber is empty

f) All of the above

24. Which are parts of the fundamentals of pistol marksmanship?

a) Grip

b) Stance

c) Sight Alignment

d) Breath Control

e) Trigger Squeeze

f) All of the above

Defensive Handgun – Review Answers

1. True

2. True

3. True

4. False

5. True

6. True

7. True

8. True

9. True

10. True

11. True

12. True

13. True

14. False

15. False

16. True

17. c

18. c

19. e

20. e

21. e

22. f

23. f

24. f

The below contact information is designed to give you a state by state listing of where you may obtain additional information on concealed carry laws, carrying a concealed weapons (CCW) applications and the issuing authority for the CCW. Please understand the information is subject to change. It is strongly recommended that you contact the appropriate authorities in the various states you frequent to become familiar with the CCW laws of those respective states; as the laws may vary tremendously from state to state.

The right to carry, reciprocity and recognition between states are subject to frequent change through either legislative action and/ or regulatory interpretation. For the best advice on concealed carry laws in the United States or in a respective state it is highly recommended that you hire an attorney in that state that specializes in Firearms law.

While there is no federal law specifically addressing the issuance of concealed carry permits, 48 states have passed laws allowing citizens to carry certain concealed firearms in public, either without a permit or after obtaining a permit from state or local law enforcement. The states give different terms for licenses or permits to carry a concealed firearm, such as:

Concealed Handgun License/Permit (CHL/CHP)

Concealed (Defensive/Deadly) Weapon Permit/License (CDWL/CWP/CWL)

Concealed Carry Permit/License (CCP/CCL)

License to Carry (Firearms) (LTC/LTCF)

Carry of Concealed Deadly Weapon License (CCDW), etc.

Also below is a listing of some additional sites which may help you obtain some additional CCW information:

National Rifle Association (NRA) - Institute of Legislative Action (ILA)www.nraila.org/gunlaws/

CarryConcealed.net

www.carryconcealed.net

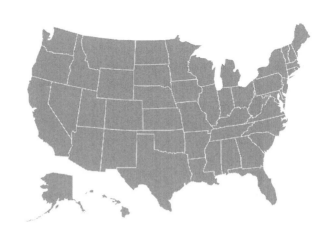

AUTHORITIES LISTED BY STATE

ALABAMA

Attorney General
Alabama State House
11 South Union Street, 3rd Floor
Montgomery, AL 36130
Phone: 334-242-7300

Alabama Dept. of Public Safety
500 Dexter Avenue
Montgomery, AL 36130
Phone: 334-242-4392
Email: info@dps.state.al.us
Issuing Authority: County Sheriff

ALASKA

Alaska Dept. of Public Safety

Permits and Licensing Unit

5700 E. Tudor Road

Anchorage, AK 99507

Phone: 907-269-0392 AK Concealed Handgun Licenses

907-269-0393 Other Permits & Licensing Programs

Fax: 907-269-5609

Issuing Authority: State Trooper

ARIZONA

Arizona Department of Public Safety

Attn: Concealed Weapons Permit Unit

P.O. Box6488

Phoenix, AZ 85005

Phone: 602-256-6280 or 800-256-6280

Fax: 602-223-2928

Email: ccw@dps.state.az.us

Arizona Attorney General

1275 W. Washington Street

Phoenix, Arizona 85007

Phone: 602-542-4266 and 888-377-6108

Issuing Authority: Arizona Department of Public Safety

ARKANSAS

Regulatory Services Division
Attn: Arkansas State Police
#1 State Police Plaza Drive
Little Rock, AR 72209-2971
Phone: 501-618-8627
Fax: 501-618-8647

Office of the Attorney General
200 Catlett-Prien Tower
323 Center Street
Little Rock, AR 72201
Phone: 501-682-1323 and 800-448-3014
Email: oag@ag.state.ar.us
Issuing Authority: State Police

CALIFORNIA

California Attorney General
Attn: Department of Justice
P.O. Box 944255
Sacramento, CA 94244-2550
Phone: 916-445-9555
Issuing Authority: County Sheriff

COLORADO

Attorney General

1525 Sherman 5th Floor

Denver, CO 80203

Phone: 303-866-4500

Fax: 303-866-5691

Email: attorney.general@state.co.us

Colorado Bureau of Investigation

690 Kipling St. Suite 3000

Denver, CO 80215

Phone: 303-239-5850

Email: james.spoden@cdps.state.co.us

Issuing Authority: County Sheriff

CONNECTICUT

Department of Public Safety

1111 Country Club Road

Middletown, CT 06450-9294

Phone: 860-685-8000

Fax: 860-685-8354

Email: DPS.Feedback@po.state.ct.us

Attorney General

55 Elm Street

Hartford, CT 06106

Phone: 860-808-5318

Fax: 860 808-5387

Email: Attorney.General@po.state.ct.us

Issuing Authority: Chief of Police

DELAWARE

Delaware State Police

P.O. Box 430

Dover, DE 9903-0430

Phone: 302-739-5900

Attorney General

Carvel State Office Building

820 N. French Street

Wilmington, DE 19801

Email: Attorney.General@State.DE.US

Issuing Authority: Prothonotary of Superior Court

FLORIDA

Florida Dept. of Agriculture and Consumer Services,

Division of Licensing

P.O. Box 6687

Tallahassee, FL 32314-6687

Phone: 850-488-5381

email: springb@doacs.state.fl.us

Office of Attorney General

State of Florida The Capital

Tallahasse, FL 32399-1050

Phone: 850-414-3300

Fax: 850-410-1630

email: ag@oag.state.fl.us

Issuing Authority: FL Dept. of Agriculture & Consumer Services

GEORGIA

Georgia Bureau of Investigation
P.O. Box 370748
Decatur, GA 30037-0748
Phone: 404-244-2501

Georgia Attorney General
40 Capitol Square, SW
Atlanta, GA 30334-1300
Phone: 404-656-3300
Issuing Authority: County Probate Judge

HAWAII

Honolulu Police Department
Attn: Firearms Division
801 S. Beretania
Honolulu, HI
Phone: 808-529-3371
Fax: 808-529-3525
hpd@honolulupd.org

Attorney General
Department of the Attorney General
425 Queen Street
Honolulu, HI 96813
Issuing Authority: Chief of Police

IDAHO

All state permits

Idaho Department of Law Enforcement

700 S. Stratford Dr

P.O. Box 700

Meridian, ID 83680-0700

Phone: 208-884-7000

Idaho Attorney General

700 W. Jefferson Street

P.O. Box 83720

Boise, ID 83720-0010

Phone: 208-334-2400

Fax: 208-334-2530

Issuing Authority: County Sheriff

INDIANA

State Police

100 North Senate Avenue

Indiana Government Center North, 3rd Floor

Indianapolis, IN 46204-2259

Phone: 317-232-8200

Indiana Attorney General

State House, Room 219

Indianapolis, IN 46204

Phone: 317-232-6201

Issuing Authority: State Police through Chief Law Enforcement
                                    Officer of Municipality

ILLINOIS

Illinois State Police
P.O. Box 19461
Springfield, IL 62794-9461
Phone: 217-782-7263
Fax: 217-785-2821

Attorney General
500 South Second St.
Springfield, IL 62706
Phone: 217-782-1090
Email: attorney_general@state.il.us

IOWA

Iowa Department of Public Safety
Wallace State Office Building
Des Moines, Iowa 50319
Phone: 515-281-3211
Email: webteam@dps.state.ia.us

Attorney General
1305 E. Walnut Street
Des Moines, Iowa 50319
Phone: 515-281-5164
Fax: 515-281-4209
Email: webteam@ag.state.ia.us
Issuing Authority: Sheriff for residents, Commissioner

KANSAS

Attorney General

301 S.W. 10th Avenue

Topeka, KS 66612-1597

Phone: 785-296-2215

Fax: 785-296-6296

Email: GENERAL@at01po.wpo.state.ks.us

Highway Patrol

General Headquarters

122 SW 7th Street

Topeka, KS 66603-3847

Phone: 785-296-6800

Fax: 785-296-3049

Issuing Authority: Attorney General

KENTUCKY

Kentucky State Police

919 Versailles Road

Frankfort, KY 40601

Phone: 502-227-8725

Office of the Kentucky Attorney General

Frankfort, KY 40601

Phone: (502) 696-5300

Issuing Authority: State Police

LOUISIANA

Louisiana State Police/Department of Public Safety

P.O. Box 66614

Baton Rouge, LA 70896-6614

Phone: 225-925-4239

Fax: 225-925-3717

Email: concealed-handguns@dps.state.la.us

Louisiana Attorney General

State Capitol, 24th Floor

P.O. Box 940005

Baton Rouge, LA 70802

Phone: 225-342-7876

Fax: 225-342-3790

http://www.ag.state.la.us

Issuing Authority: Department of Public Safety & Corrections

MAINE

Department of Public Safety

Maine State Police, Licensing Division

45 Commerce Dr.

Augusta, ME. 04333

Phone: 207-624-7210

Attorney General

6 State House Station

Augusta, ME 04333

Phone: 207-626-8800

http://www.me.state.us.ag/homepage.htm

Issuing Authority: Chief of Police

MARYLAND

Maryland State Police
Attn: Handgun Permit Section
7751 Washington Blvd
Jessup, MD 20794
Phone: 410-486-3101

Attorney General
200 St. Paul Place
Baltimore, MD 21202
Phone: 410-576-6300
Fax: 410-576-6447
Issuing Authority: Superintendent of State Police

MASSACHUSETTS

Firearms Records Bureau
Attn: Firearms License
200 Arlington Street
Suite 2200
Chelsea, MA 02150
Phone: 617-660-4780

Massachusetts State Police
470 Worcester Road
Framingham, Massachusetts 01702
Phone: 508-820-2300
Email: msp.webmaster@pol.state.ma.us
Issuing Authority: Department of State Police,
                      Firearms Record Bureau

MICHIGAN

Michigan Department of State Police

714 S. Harrison Road

East Lansing, MI 48823

Phone: 517-332-2521

Michigan Attorney General

525 W Ottawa Street

Lansing, MI 48909

Phone: 517-373-1110

Fax: 517-241-1850

http://www.ag.state.mi.us

Issuing Authority: County Gun Board/Sheriff

MINNESOTA

Minnesota Department of Public Safety

444 Cedar Street

Saint Paul, MN 55101

Phone: 651-282-6565

bca.permitstocarry@state.mn.us

Minnesota Attorney General

102 State Capitol

St. Paul, MN 55155

Phone: 651-296-6196

Fax: 651-297-4193

http://www.ag.state.mn.us

Issuing Authority: Chief of Police/County Sheriff

MISSISSIPPI

Mississippi State Police

P. O. Box 958

Jackson, MS 39205-0958

Phone: 601-987-1212

Email: jtucker@dps.state.ms.us

Attorney General

P.O. Box 220

Jackson, MS 39205-0220

Phone: 601-987-1586

http://www.ago.state.ms.us

Issuing Authority: Department of Public Safety/Highway Patrol

MISSOURI

Department of Public Safety

P.O. Box 749

Jefferson City, MO 65102-0749

Phone: 573-751-4905

Fax: 573-751-5399

Attorney General

Supreme Court Building 207 W. High St

P.O. Box 899

Jefferson City, MO 65102

Phone: 573-751-3321

Fax: 573-751-0774

http://www.ago.state.mo.us

Issuing Authority: County Sheriff

MONTANA

Attorney General Mike McGrath

Department of Justice

P.O. Box 201401

Helena, MT 59620-1401

Phone: 406-444-2026

Fax: 406-444-3549

E-mail: contactdoj@mt.gov

Issuing Authority: County Sheriff

NEBRASKA

Nebraska State Patrol

P.O. Box 94907

Lincoln, NE 68509

Phone: 402-471-4545

Attorney General

2115 State Capitol

P.O. Box 98920

Lincoln, NE 68509-8920

Phone: 402-471-2682

Fax: 402-471-3297

Issuing Authority: Nebraska State Police

NEVADA

Office of the Attorney General

100 N. Carson Street

Carson City, NV 89701-4717

Phone: 775-684-1100

Fax: 775-684-1108

Email: aginfo@ag.state.nv.us

Issuing Authority: County Sheriff

NEW HAMPSHIRE

Director of State Police

Permits and Licensing Unit

35 Hazen Drive

Concord, NH 03305

Phone: 603-271-3575

Fax: 603-271-1153

Issuing Authority: Selectman/Mayor or Chief of Police

NEW JERSEY

New Jersey State Police Firearms Investigation Unit

PO Box 7068

West Trenton, NJ 08628-0068

Phone: 609-882-2000 ext. 2664

Office of the Attorney General
Dept. of Law & Public Safety
P.O. Box 080
Trenton, NJ 08625-0080
Phone: 609-292-4925
Fax: 609-292-3508
http://www.njpublicsafety.com
Issuing Authority: Chief of Police/Superintendent of State Police

NEW MEXICO

Department of Public Safety
P.O. Box 1628
Santa Fe, NM 87504
Phone: 505-841-8053 ext. 1127
http://www.dps.nm.org/

Attorney General
407 Galisteo Street
Bataan Memorial Building, Rm 260
Santa Fe, NM 87501
Phone: 505-827-6000
Fax: 505-827-5826
http://www.ago.state.nm.us
Issuing Authority: Department of Public Safety

NEW YORK

State Police

Counsel's Office

Bldg. 22, 1220 Washington Ave.

Albany, NY 12226

Phone: 518-457-6811

Attorney General

120 Broadway

New York, NY 10271-0332

Phone: 212-416-8000

http://www.oag.state.ny.us

Issuing Authority: Varies by county

NORTH CAROLINA

North Carolina Highway Patrol

512 N. Salisbury Street

4702 Mail Service Center

Raleigh, NC 27699-4702

Phone: 919-733-7952

Email: Webmaster@ncshp.org

Attorney General

North Carolina Department of Justice

P.O. Box 629

Raleigh, NC 27602-0629

Phone: 919-716-6400

Fax: 919-716-6750

Email: agjus@mail.jus.state.nc.us

Issuing Authority: County Sheriff

NORTH DAKOTA

Chief of the Bureau of Criminal Investigation

Bureau of Criminal Investigation

Bismarck, ND 58502-1054

Phone: 701-328-5500

Fax: 701-328-5510

Email: bciinfo@state.nd.us

North Dakota Office of Attorney General

Office of Attorney General

State Capitol

600 E Boulevard Ave. Dept 125

Bismarck, ND 58505-0040

Phone: 701-328-2210

Fax: 701-328-2226

Email: ndag@state.nd.us

Issuing Authority: Chief of the Bureau of Criminal Investigation

OHIO

Ohio Highway Patrol

P O Box 182074

Columbus, OH 43232

http://www.state.oh.us/ohiostatepatrol

Attorney General

30 E. Broad Street 17th Floor

Columbus, OH 43215-3428

Phone: 614-466-4320

Fax: 614-466-5057

Issuing Authority: County Sheriff

OKLAHOMA

Oklahoma State Bureau of Investigation

6600 N. Harvey Suite 300

Oklahoma City, OK 73116

Phone: 405-848-6724 or 800-207-6724 outside Oklahoma City

sda@osbi.state.ok.us

Attorney General

112 State Capitol

2300 N. Lincoln Blvd.

Oklahoma City, OK 73105

Phone: 405-521-3921

Fax: 405-521-6246

http://www.oag.state.of.us

Issuing Authority: State Bureau of Investigation

OREGON

State Police

400 Public Service Bldg., 255 Capitol St. N.E.

Salem, OR 97310

Phone: 503-378-3720

Fax: 503-378-8282

http://www.osp.state.or.us

Attorney General/Justice Department

1162 Court St. NE

Salem Oregon, 97310

Phone: 503-378-4400

Fax: 503-378-5938

http://www.doj.state.or.us

Issuing Authority: County Sherriff

PENNSYLVANIA

State Police

1800 Elmerton Avenue

Harrisburg, PA 17110-9758

Phone: 717-783-5599

Fax: 717-787-2948

Attorney General

16th Floor, Strawberry Square

Harrisburg, PA 17120

Phone: 717-787-3391

Fax: 717-787-8242

http://www.attorneygeneral.gov

Issuing Authority: County Sheriff or Chief of Police

RHODE ISLAND

State Police

311 Danielson Pike

North Scituate, RI 02857

Phone: 401-444-1000

Fax: 401-444-1105

http://www.risp.state.ri.us

Attorney General

150 South Main Street

Providence, RI 02903

Phone: 401-274-4400

Fax: 401-222-1331

http://www.riag.state.ri.us

Issuing Authority: Attorney General

SOUTH CAROLINA

South Carolina Law Enforcement Division
Attn: Regulatory Services Unit
P.O. Box 21398
Columbia, SC 29221
Phone: 803-896-7014

Attorney General
Box 11549
Columbia, SC 29211
Phone: 803-734-3970
Fax: 803-253-6283
http://www.scattorneygeneral.org
Issuing Authority: S.C. Law Enforcement Division

SOUTH DAKOTA

Highway Patrol
118 West Capitol
Pierre, SD 57501
Phone: 605-773-3105
Fax: 605-773-6046
http://hp.state.sd.us/information.htm

Attorney General
500 East Capitol Ave.
Pierre, SD 57501-5070
Phone: 605-773-3215
Fax: 605-773-4106
http://www.state.sd.attorney/office/news/concealed.asp
Issuing Authority: Chief of Police/County Sheriff/Sec of State

TENNESSEE

Tennessee Department of Safety
Attn: Handgun Carry Permit Office
1150 Foster Ave
Nashville, TN 37249-1000
Phone: 615-251-8590

Attorney General
P.O. Box 20207
Nashville, TN 37202
Phone: 615-741-3491
Fax: 615-741-2009
http://www.attorneygeneral.state.tn.us
Issuing Authority: Dept of Public Safety, Handgun Carry Permit

TEXAS

Texas Department of Public Safety
Concealed Handgun Licensing Section
P O Box 4143
Austin, TX 78791-4143
Phone: 512-424-7293 or 800-224-5744
http://www.txdps.state.tx.us

Attorney General
P. O. Box 12548
Austin, TX 78711-2548
Phone: 512-463-2100
Fax: 512-463-2063
http://www.oag.state.tx.us
Issuing Authority: Department of Public Safety

UTAH

UT Dept of Public Safety Bureau of Criminal Identification
3888 W. 5400 S.
P.O. Box 148280
Salt Lake City, UT 84114-8280
Phone: 801-965-4445

Utah Attorney General
236 State Capitol
Salt Lake City, Utah 84114
Phone: 801-366-0260
Fax: 801-538-1121
http://www.attorneygeneral.utah.gov

Issuing Authority: Dept of Public Safety, UT Bureau of Criminal Identification

VERMONT

Attorney General
109 State Street
Montpelier, VT 05609-1001
Phone: 802-828 3171
Fax: 802-828 2154

VIRGINIA

Virginia State Police
P.O. Box 27472
Richmond, VA 23261
Phone: 804-674-2000

Attorney General
900 East Main Street
Richmond, VA 23219
Phone: 804-786-2071
Fax: 804-786-1991
http://www.oag.state.va.us
Issuing Authority: State Circuit Court of residence

WASHINGTON

Washington State Patrol
General Administration Building
PO Box 42600
Olympia, WA 98504-2600
Phone: 360-753-6540
Fax: 360-753-2492

Attorney General
1125 Washington St. SE
Olympia, WA 98504-0100
Phone: 360-753-6200
Fax: 360-664-0988
http://www.atg.wa.gov
Issuing Authority: Chief of Police/Sheriff

WASHINGTON, DC

Government of the District of Columbia

Citywide Call Center

John A. Wilson Building

1350 Pennsylvania Avenue, NW

Washington, DC 20004

Phone: 202-727-1000

Issuing Authority: Chief of Police

WEST VIRGINIA

West Virginia State Police

725 Jefferson Road

South Charleston, WV 25309

Phone: 304-746-2100

Fax: 304-746-2246

Attorney General - is responsible for CCW, new for 2007

State Capitol, Room 26-E

1900 Kanawha Blvd.

East Charleston, WV 25305-0220

Phone: 304-558-2021

Fax: 304-558-0140

http://www.state.wv.us/wvag/

http://www.wvago.gov/gunrecep.cfm

Issuing Authority: County Sheriff

WISCONSIN

Attorney General

123 West Washington Ave.

PO Box 7857

Madison, WI 53707-7857

Phone: 608-266-1221

Fax: 608-267-2779

WYOMING

Wyoming Attorney General's Office

123 Capitol Building

200 W. 24th Street

Cheyenne, WY 82002

Phone: 307-777-7841

Fax: 307-777-6869

Issuing Authority: Attorney General

Email: webteam@ag.state.ia.us

Issuing Authority: Sheriff for residents, Commissioner

CRITICAL GEORGIA FIREARM CODES

At the conclusion of this section you will understand key Georgia Firearm Codes. They will also understand three situations which justify the use of deadly force:

- Defense of self from great bodily harm or death

- Defense of a third person from great bodily harm or death

- To prevent the commission of a forcible felony

§ 16-1-3. Definitions

§ 16-3-21 Use of force in defense of self or others; evidence of belief that force was necessary in murder or manslaughter prosecution

§ 16-3-23 Use of force in defense of habitation

Definitions

25.

   § 16-1-3. Definitions

   As used in this title, the term:

   (1) "Affirmative defense" means, with respect to any affirmative defense authorized in this title, unless the state's evidence raises the issue invoking the alleged defense, the defendant must present evidence thereon to raise the issue. The enumeration in this title of some affirmative defenses shall

not be construed as excluding the existence of others.

(2) "Agency" means:

(A) When used with respect to the state government, any department, commission, committee, authority, board, or bureau thereof; and

(B) When used with respect to any political subdivision of the state government, any department, commission, committee, authority, board, or bureau thereof.

(3) "Another" means a person or persons other than the accused.

(4) "Conviction" includes a final judgment of conviction entered upon a verdict or finding of guilty of a crime or upon a plea of guilty.

(5) "Felony" means a crime punishable by death, by imprisonment for life, or by imprisonment for more than 12 months.

(6) "Forcible felony" means any felony which involves the use or threat of physical force or violence against any person.

(7) "Forcible misdemeanor" means any misdemeanor which involves the use or threat of physical force or violence against any person.

(8) "Government" means the United States, the state, any political subdivision thereof, or any agency of the foregoing.

(9) "Misdemeanor" and "misdemeanor of a high and aggravated nature" mean any crime other than a felony.

(10) "Owner" means a person who has a right to possession of property which is superior to that of a person who takes, uses, obtains, or withholds it from him and which the person taking, using, obtaining, or withholding is not privileged to infringe.

(11) "Peace officer" means any person who by virtue of his office or public employment is vested by law with a duty to maintain public order or to make arrests for offenses, whether that duty extends to all crimes or is limited to specific offenses.

(12) "Person" means an individual, a public or private corporation, an incorporated association, government, government agency, partnership, or unincorporated association.

(13) "Property" means anything of value, including but not limited to real estate, tangible and intangible personal property, contract rights, services, choses in action, and other interests in or claims to wealth, admission or transportation tickets, captured or domestic animals, food and drink, and electric or other power.

(14) "Prosecution" means all legal proceedings by which a person's liability for a crime is determined, commencing with the return of the indictment or the filing of the accusation, and including the final disposition of the case upon appeal.

(15) "Public place" means any place where the conduct involved may reasonably be expected to be viewed by people other than members of the actor's family or household.

(16) "Reasonable belief" means that the person concerned, acting as a

reasonable man, believes that the described facts exist.

(17) "State" means the State of Georgia, all land and water in respect to which this state has either exclusive or concurrent jurisdiction, and the airspace above such land and water.

(18) "Without authority" means without legal right or privilege or without permission of a person legally entitled to withhold the right.

(19) "Without his consent" means that a person whose concurrence is required has not, with knowledge of the essential facts, voluntarily yielded to the proposal of the accused or of another.

USE OF FORCE IN DEFENSE OF SELF OR OTHERS

§ 16-3-21

(a) A person is justified in threatening or using force against another when and to the extent that he or she reasonably believes that such threat or force is necessary to defend himself or herself or a third person against such other's imminent use of unlawful force; however, except as provided in Code Section 16-3-23, *a person is justified in using force which is intended or likely to cause death or great bodily harm only if he or she reasonably believes that such force is necessary to prevent death or great bodily injury to himself or herself or a third person or to prevent the commission of a forcible felony.*

(b) A person is not justified in using force under the circumstances specified in subsection (a) of this Code section if he:

(1) Initially provokes the use of force against himself with the intent to use such force as an excuse to inflict bodily harm upon the assailant;

(2) Is attempting to commit, committing, or fleeing after the commission or attempted commission of a felony; or

(3) Was the aggressor or was engaged in a combat by agreement unless he withdraws from the encounter and effectively communicates to such other person his intent to do so and the other, notwithstanding, continues or threatens to continue the use of unlawful force.

(c) Any rule, regulation, or policy of any agency of the state or any ordinance, resolution, rule, regulation, or policy of any county, municipality, or other political subdivision of the state which is in conflict with this Code section shall be null, void, and of no force and effect.

(d) In a prosecution for murder or manslaughter, if a defendant raises as a defense a justification provided by subsection (a) of this Code section, the defendant, in order to establish the defendant's reasonable belief that the use of force or deadly force was immediately necessary, may be permitted to offer:

(1) Relevant evidence that the defendant had been the victim of acts of family violence or child abuse committed by the deceased, as such acts are described in Code Sections 19-13-1 and 19-15-1, respectively; and

(2) Relevant expert testimony regarding the condition of the mind of the defendant at the time of the offense, including those relevant facts and circumstances relating to the family violence or child abuse that are the bases of the expert's opinion.

Use of force in Defense of Habitation

§ 16-3-23

A person is justified in threatening or using force against another when and to the extent that he or she reasonably believes that such threat or force is necessary to prevent or terminate such other's unlawful entry into or attack upon a habitation; however, such person is justified in the use of force which is intended or likely to cause death or great bodily harm only if:

(1) The entry is made or attempted in a violent and tumultuous manner and he or she reasonably believes that the entry is attempted or made for the purpose of assaulting or offering personal violence to any person dwelling or being therein and that such force is necessary to prevent the assault or offer of personal violence;

(2) That force is used against another person who is not a member of the

family or household and who unlawfully and forcibly enters or has unlawfully and forcibly entered the residence and the person using such force knew or had reason to believe that an unlawful and forcible entry occurred; or

(3) The person using such force reasonably believes that the entry is made or attempted for the purpose of committing a felony therein and that such force is necessary to prevent the commission of the felony.

INDEX

6148121R0

Made in the USA
Charleston, SC
19 September 2010